# THE POEMS OF

# Celia Thaxter

*Celia Laighton Thaxter in her island garden, Appledore*
*Courtesy University of New Hampshire*

# THE POEMS OF
# Celia Thaxter

## INTRODUCTION BY
## JANE E. VALLIER

PETER E. RANDALL
PUBLISHER
PORTSMOUTH, NH
1996

© *Introduction 1996 by Jane E. Vallier*
*Printed in the United States of America*

*Cover design by Tom Allen*

*ISBN 0-91439-57-5*

*Peter E. Randall Publisher*
*Box 4726, Portsmouth, NH 03802*

*This volume is a reprint of* The Poems of Celia Thaxter, Appledore Edition, *published by Houghton, Mifflin and Company in 1896, plus selections from* The Heavenly Guest, *published by Oscar Laighton in 1935, and* Stories and Poems for Children, *published by Houghton, Mifflin and Company in 1895.*

*To the memory of Celia Laighton Thaxter*

*"...There was something bright in her spirit that
will forever shine and light the hearts of those who
loved her."*

      *Sarah Orne Jewett*

  *We "wore your roses yesterday," dear Celia,
and now on the one hundredth anniversary of the
publication of the Appledore edition of your collected
poems, we reissue this volume, "and every thought
of you a rose."*

     *Faye Labanaris/Peter Randall*

# CONTENTS

*Celia Thaxter, 1887*
*Courtesy Portsmouth Public Library*

# The World of Celia Thaxter

## Part I: "My Lighthouse"

CELIA LAIGHTON THAXTER, the most widely published woman writing poetry in America in the last half of the nineteenth century, lived a life of mythic dimensions. Born in Portsmouth, New Hampshire, on June 29, 1835 to Thomas and Eliza (Rymes) Laighton, Celia developed into a woman who came to embody all that American women of her time could hope to achieve without the support of wealth, position, or even good fortune. Her life was a triumph of the human spirit over adversity, of courage over despair.

In 1839, four-year old Celia, along with her parents and younger brother Oscar, journeyed ten miles out into the Atlantic to a rocky promontory known as White Island, where her father would become the lighthouse keeper and where he would eventually build a resort domain in the Isles of Shoals. Another brother, Cedric, was born in 1840. The four years when the family lived on the tiny lighthouse island were to become, in Celia's mind, the mythic source from which all of her life and art were formed, and from which all of her writing drew. Unrestrained by formal education and stifling female role models, Celia spoke to the waves and the birds and the clouds—as well as to her two younger brothers—with an unfettered imagination and with a genius for language. Precocious and unspoiled, little Celia felt a mystic bond with nature. Thirty years later she wrote:

> Ever I longed to speak these things that made life so sweet, to speak the wind, the cloud, and the bird's flight, the sea's murmur...but the wish ever grew. Facing the July sunsets, deep red and golden through and through, or watching the summer northern lights,—battalions of brilliant streamers advancing and retreating, shooting upward to the zenith, and flowing like fiery veils before the stars; or when the fog bow spanned the silver mist of morning, or the earth and sea lay shimmering in a gold-

9

*Celia Thaxter at age twenty-one*
*Courtesy Portsmouth Public Library*

en haze of noon; in storm or calm, by day or night, the manifold aspect of Nature held me and swayed all my thoughts until it was impossible to be silent any longer, and I was fain to mingle my voice with her myriad voices, only aspiring to be in accord with the Infinite harmony, however feeble and broken the notes might be.

*Among the Isles of Shoals*, 141-43

And, that is the story of Celia's early childhood, filled as it must have been with legends of the sea, tales shipwrecks and disasters, and the iambic pentameter of Shakespeare and the Psalms. She remained all of her life a poet of the oral tradition—a poet of sounds and music, of birds' singing and of the wind's and ocean's roar. As her poetic consciousness developed, she began to hope that the infallible messages of her five senses would become paths to reason, but in the end, some fifty years later when she intuited her own death, she had by then arrived at a faith which was beyond what she could see, hear, smell, or touch. She heard her own voice in the wind and waves, and they called her to an heroic life.

In 1843, when Celia was only eight, Levi Thaxter, a recent Harvard Law School graduate and aspiring actor, came to the White Island lighthouse to "rusticate," to enjoy nature in a leisurely setting as many of his fellow transcendentalists were doing. He became enamored of the Thaxter children, the precocious Celia, and her two younger brothers, Oscar then four and Cedric just three, and in a free-spirited manner, volunteered to become their tutor. He delighted the children with stories and with the scientific exploration of their island, and he brought to them the gift of the Boston Brahmin culture. Levi's visits were sporadic, however, with Mr. Laighton assuming the responsibility for the children's education in mathematics.

By 1847, Mr. Thaxter and Mr. Laighton had decided to become business partners in a resort hotel venture on Appledore, another island at the Isles of Shoals, and their partnership seemed to seal the fate of the blossoming young Celia. The next year she and Levi were engaged, and although the hotel partnership dissolved, the marriage took place on September 30, 1851 in a family ceremony at the Appledore Hotel. What appeared to be at first the fairy tale rescue of an island princess by a Boston Brahmin prince did not end, with "happily ever after." During the first year while the young couple lived on Star Island with Levi serving as minister and schoolmaster, Celia experienced the only relatively care-free time in their marriage. The story of the Thaxter marriage is one of beset by tragedy, as several biographers including Celia's granddaughter have written. Within the first year, Karl Thaxter was born, handicapped by a birth injury or a brain disorder that would require his mother's constant care for the rest of his life. A second son, John, was born the next year, and with two babies, Celia's childhood closed forever. A third son, Roland, was born in 1858, by which time the family had settled in an old farmhouse in Newtonville, Massachusetts, near Levi's parents' home in Watertown. There the young couple were in close contact with Levi's Harvard friends including James and Maria Lowell, Thomas Wentworth Higginson, William Morris Hunt, and John Weiss, as well as the Concord transcendentalists who lived at the center of American literature and culture. Celia flourished in the social world of Brahmin Boston, but at the same time felt beleaguered by housekeeping and care of three children as well as the uncertainties raised by her eccentric and unemployed husband. Perhaps Levi had underestimated the capacity for intellectual and social development in the child he had found to be so precocious. Nathaniel Hawthorne had described her as an "Island Miranda," so taken he was with her beauty and her musical inclinations.

Celia's first poem, "Land-locked," was published in the *Atlantic* March, 1861. Since her name was not listed as the author, some people thought Levi had written the poem. However, as more poems in the same voice appeared regularly, Celia became recognized as the author within a couple of years. By 1872, her first volume, *Poems,* met with the enthusiasm of her reading public. Although the copyright was in Levi's name, Celia had been launched as a female poetic voice in New England. The next year, 1873, Celia's childhood reminiscence, *Among the Isles of Shoals* became one of the three best selling books in America for her publisher, Houghton Mifflin.

In spite of her publishing success and her growing reputation as a writer, the decade of the 1870s was a difficult one for Celia. She left the Newtonville house in 1872 to care for her ailing mother at the Shoals, Levi traveled extensively seeking better health and ornithological specimens, and Karl reached a precarious adulthood, unable to survive without his mother's constant supervision. Sons John and Roland often accompanied Levi, thus leaving the family separated. The distinguished painter, William Morris Hunt, Levi's comrade and soul mate, often made his home in the Newtonville house where Celia had once presided. Returned to her childhood home now on a year around basis, Celia wrote a second , enlarged edition of *Poems* (1874) and third volume, *Driftweed* (1878). Although her fame was rising, Celia was lonely and adrift except during the summer seasons when the Appledore Hotel, now managed by her brothers, brought cultured vacationers to the windswept islands. The death of her beloved mother in 1877 brought Celia to a crisis of artistic development and religious faith whereupon she turned to spiritualism and Eastern religions.

In 1880, Celia sought inspiration and renewal in a trip to Europe with her brother, Oscar. Letters written to Annie Fields, John Greenleaf Whittier, Sarah Orne Jewett, and other literary friends reveal an American writer comfortably familiar with European culture. The highlight for Celia was a visit with Robert Browning. When she returned to America, writing for children's magazines such as *Our Young Folks*, *St. Nicholas*, and *Wide Awake*, cultivating her garden on Appledore, and serving as the hostess of an artistic circle during the summer season at the Shoals occupied Celia's time. The Thaxter family sold the house in Newtonville and bought a farm at Kittery Point in 1881; but not even Levi's declining health could reconcile the marriage, and he died there in 1884. John Thaxter took over the farm which supplied milk and butter to the hotel, while Celia and Karl lived at the Shoals in summer and wintered in Portsmouth. Celia published *Stories and Poems for Children* in 1883, by which time she was recognized as one of the best writers of children's literature in America. *The Cruise of the Mystery and Other Poems* followed in 1886; then came *Pastorals and Idylls* in 1888, and *Verses* in 1891.

As the 1880s came to a close, Celia was being celebrated as the hostess of her literary and artistic circle. Her flower-filled salon in the cottage at Appledore welcomed writers, painters and musicians—the best in American culture. In addition to writers such as Sarah Orne Jewett, Annie Fields, Rose Lamb, Sarah Whitman and Elizabeth Stuart Phelps, John Greenleaf Whittier, and William Dean Howells, Celia attracted painters such as Childe Hassam, Ellen Robbins, J. Appleton Brown, and Ross Turner to paint the splendor of the Isles

*Celia Thaxter's cottage parlor on Appledore where she worked and entertained her many friends. Courtesy Portsmouth Public Library*

and the glory of her garden. Musicians from Harvard and Boston composed art songs and symphonies under her influence. Piano sonatas drifted from the parlor to mingle with the wind and the waves. It is not surprising that what might be called a "Cult of Beauty" developed around Celia as she became the mentor to a younger generations of musicians, artists and writers (See bibliography of Thaxter songs).

Although she had suffered a heart attack in 1889, she appeared to be in good health as the 1890s began. The writing of *An Island Garden* (1894) was uncharacteristically difficult for her, however, and she was compelled to rely on Sarah Orne Jewett, her beloved friend from South Berwick, Maine, to assist in the editing. Boston book designer and artist Sarah W. Whitman designed an elegant cover, and Childe Hassam's watercolors made the volume an artistic treasure. It seemed that, at the age of 59, Celia had reached her artistic stride. No one was prepared for her sudden death on August 26, 1894 at the height of the summer season on Appledore—except perhaps Celia herself. Just a few weeks before her death, she took Sarah Jewett, Annie Fields, and other dear friends on a tour of the islands, as if she were saying a personal farewell to her beloved Isles of Shoals. She died "in accord with the Infinite Harmony" that she had intuited as a child, that she had written about as a poet, and that she had exemplified heroically in her daily life.

After Celia was buried on Appledore beside her parents, the spirit of the islands seemed to dissipate. Four years later her brother Cedric died just as unexpectedly: without his financial genius and without her inspiring presence, the Laighton dream began to fade. By the turn of the century the hotel was in financial disarray, and after a few attempts to save the enterprise, it came to a disastrous end. In September of 1914, when all of the vacationers had left Appledore for the season, a fire demolished the hotel, Celia's cottage and garden, and many of the other summer residences on Appledore. Although Oscar Laighton lived to be 99-years old and was dearly loved as a benevolent presence, the tourist industry never revived, and the Isles of Shoals moved into a new era of history.

At the turn of the century, New England Unitarians had begun having summer conferences on Star Island in the Oceanic Hotel then owned by the Laightons. In 1915, the Unitarians bought both Star Island and the Oceanic Hotel and developed a summer retreat and conference center which is still in operation. Meanwhile Appledore Island and most of its property was used by the Coast Guard during World War II, and thereafter developed into the Shoals Marine Laboratory, an undergraduate field marine science teaching facility jointly sponsored by Cornell University and University of New Hampshire. Today, tours of Appledore and Star Island are available in the summers, and both islands are deeply committed to historical and environmental preservation. The White Island Lighthouse is still operated by the Coast Guard although it became automated in 1984. Limited access to the lighthouse is available today through the New Hampshire State Division of Parks.

In the seventeenth and eighteenth centuries, the Isles of Shoals had been a hardy fishing community. In the nineteenth century, the islands were a thriving resort and artist colony where urban-weary Americans could rest and renew themselves. In the twentieth century, the Isles made the transition into the Information Age by becoming a center for environmental research and religious and artistic education. As the twenty-first century approaches, these mythic islands continue to fill our human aspirations. Our needs do indeed change, but the beauty and inspirational qualities of the Isles of Shoals remain.

## Part II: The Music and the Myth

Upon Celia's death, the female literary circle of which she had been a vibrant member moved quickly to memorialize her with three books: *Poems*, the "Appledore Edition" (1896) edited by Sarah Orne Jewett; *Letters* (1896) edited by Annie Fields, Rose Lamb and Jewett; and *Stories and Poems for Children* (1895) edited by Jewett. All copyrights were held by Roland Thaxter, Celia's youngest son who was a distinguished Harvard professor of mycology. At the centenary of Celia's birth in 1935, her granddaughter, Rosamond Thaxter, and Celia's brother Oscar Laighton assembled a group of unpublished poems and tributes entitled *The Heavenly Guest*. Not until 1962 was there a biography of Celia Thaxter, whereupon granddaughter Rosamond Thaxter, one of the keepers of the family stories and treasures, wrote *Sandpiper: The Life and Letters of Celia Thaxter*. A decade later with the feminist literary renaissance of the 1970s, Celia and her circle were rediscovered as important voices in American literary history.

Celia Thaxter's soul seemed to brim with lyric poetry. Her songs, ballads, and sonnets were cries of the heart overheard by an accepting audience, an audience familiar with the old Protestant hymns, the ballads of sailors, and the narrative reassurance of the Fireside poets. As critic Northrup Frye points out, the lyric poem is "overheard" by a concealed audience. In Thaxter's lyrics, we often see her standing at the edge of the sea, and we hear her as a secular oracle whose mind hovers on the brink of the unconscious. The chaos of wind and water evoke pity and terror; then the poet takes us, through a tight metrical system to a moment of epiphany. What the poet comes to understand is seldom the answer that she wants to hear. The poems are often dramatic monologues where the poet concentrates her senses in order to fathom the meaning of existence as seen in "At the Breakers' Edge:"

Through the wide sky thy north wind's thunder roars
    Restless, till no cloud is left to flee,
And down the clear, cold heaven unhindered pours
    Thine awful moonlight on the winter sea.

The vast, black, raging spaces, torn and wild,
    With an insensate fury answer back
To the gale's challenge: hurrying breakers, piled
    Each over each, roll through the glittering track.

I shudder in the terror of thy cold,
    As buffeted by the fierce blast I stand,
Watching that shining path of bronzed gold,
    With solemn, shadowy rocks on either hand:

A poet of eye and ear, Thaxter continues to delineate the storm's fury, seeking some answer from the masculine spirit of the gale. However, as in most Thaxter poems, that voice refuses to answer the mortal question. To resolve the agony, the unanswered poet turns to a female personification of Patience for solace:

Ah! what am I, thine atom, standing here
    In presence of they pitiless elements,
Daring to question thy great silence drear,
    No voice my break to lighten our suspense!

Thou only, infinite Patience, that endures
    Forever! Blind and dumb I cling to Thee!
Slow glides the bitter night, and silent pours
    Thine awful moonlight on the winter sea.

Just as Levi Thaxter withheld his approval of his young wife's early poems, the God that Celia Thaxter depicts allows his children to suffer. Often in her early poems, Celia speaks in the voice of a child so as to mask her despair. In "Watching" we hear this young voice which is slightly reminiscent of Huckleberry Finn's whistling as he passed the graveyard:

> I will be patient now,
> Dear Heavenly Father, waiting here for Thee:
> I know the darkness holds Thee. Shall I be
> Afraid, then it Thou?
>
> On thy eternal shore,
> In pauses, when life's tide is at its prime,
> I hear the everlasting rote of Time
> Beating for evermore.
>
> Shall not I then rejoice?
> Oh, never lost or sad should child of thine
> Sit waiting, fearing lest there come no sign,
> No whisper of thy voice!

Little has been written about Celia's grounding in the Greek litera-
ture of which Levi was a recognized scholar. Celia even painted Greek
inscriptions on some of the china that she decorated with olive leaves
and branches. Whether or not she knew the language, she spent many
hours with Annie Fields, also a Greek scholar and translator, reading
aloud and discussing world literature. The islands of epic Greek tales
must have informed her vision of her own island home, and her unwa-
vering acceptance of Fate kept her from embracing Christianity until
the last few years of her life. Aristotelian catharsis and the Longinean
sublime can be found and most of her poems. Nonetheless, she saw
"the beautiful" in birds, flowers and the faces of children, but she
knew that they were only temporary stays against an indifferent uni-
verse. Occasionally a rhapsodic moment occurs at sunrise or sunset,
between calm and storm, and she stores up the treasured memory for
the inevitable torrent that is to come. An American Calypso, Celia
Thaxter never expected to be rescued.

Women, in the American literary tradition, have spent their lives
on the shore, at the terrifying edge of their own consciousness, wait-
ing for a sign of hope, a sail in the distance, a familiar voice. They are
realists, however: Sarah Orne Jewett, Harriet Beecher Stowe, Mary
Wilkins Freeman, Lucy Larcom, Elizabeth Stuart Phelps, Elizabeth
Stoddard—and even Emily Dickinson who wrote:

Adrift! A little boat adrift!
And night is coming down!
Will no one guide this little boat
Unto the nearest town?

#30

Only in the fantasies of the romantic young girl is the ocean a source of beauty and hope where she might sail away with her beloved. Thaxter's second published poem, "Off Shore" uses this rare image:

The waves are full of whispers wild and sweet;
They call to me,—incessantly they beat
Along the boat from stern to curved prow.

Romance serves as a central theme in only a few Thaxter poems; it is topic with which she was always ill at ease. The gaunt older women of Jewett's and Thaxter's later work are resigned to losing their battles with the sea. Both were unsparing realists.

Thaxter aspired to be drawn into "to the heart of nature," but her nature worship was hard won, unsentimental, and not at the expense of her adult awareness of the sea's indifference and its capacity to bend, to break, to annihilate. Out of these contradictions she created her artistic voice....

*Springer*, 1995, 201

Celia Thaxter could sing about the sea in its peaceful moods, but she never trusted its masculine fury or its seductive sunsets.

## Part III: The Tides of American Literary History

The conquest of water and land has been one of the epic themes of American literature for male writers. For female writers the epic journey has always been inward, an attempt to tame the wilderness of their own feelings and experiences. While Thoreau traveled much in Concord and up the inland waterways of the Merrimack, Emily Dickinson and her contemporary, Celia Thaxter, gardened, and baked and tended the sick and dying. Thoreau, Dickinson, and Thaxter saw the same stars wheeling above them, they listened to the same words of American wisdom from Emerson, and they struggled with the same Puritan obsession with their own souls. They asked about their place in the universe, and they came to similar answers: Thoreau's Walden Pond, Dickinson's mysterious "circumference," and Thaxter's discipline of beauty. In splendid isolation, all three sought the company of the bee, the butterfly and the breeze. Birds were their oracles, and God was ominously silent.

One of the ironies for twentieth century Thaxter scholars was the fact that she probably did not know of Emily Dickinson. Celia's husband and tutor, Levi Thaxter, was the first cousin and college roommate of Thomas Wentworth Higginson, Emily Dickinson's editor and mentor. Emily undoubtedly read Celia's poems as they appeared several times a year in the *Atlantic*. During Dickinson's poetic fury of 1862 and 1863, the *Atlantic* was featuring Thaxter's verses about the sea and island life. Although Dickinson's isolation was of a different nature, both women struggled with mental illness: Thaxter attempting to create a safe world for her mentally disabled son, Karl, and Dickinson fighting whatever demons rallied in her own mind. The Civil War, which raged some distance from New England, was mirrored in each woman's own soul.

In the midst of latter nineteenth century literary America, Celia Thaxter held a beloved and respected place. Like Mark Twain, Sarah Orne Jewett, Harriet Beecher Stowe, Thomas Bailey Aldrich, and John Greenleaf Whittier, Celia wrote for children as well as adults. Her realistic stories for the juvenile magazines never sentimentalized nature: she herself was a respected naturalist and a founder of the Audubon Society. As a personality, she was respected as a truth-teller, an open soul whose sympathy with the common lot of human suffering ennobled all whose life she touched. During the summer season on Appledore, she was a celebrity, whose words, whose nod of approval, whose autograph was eagerly sought.

A legendary beauty in her youth, a symbol of personal integrity in her mature years, Celia Thaxter spoke with a poetic voice that was true and clear. Her writing reminded us all of springtime rebirth, of the ebb and flow time, and she drew on the immense and venerable stock of responses to nature that continue to be culturally encoded in myth. For that reason alone, her poetry should survive into the twenty-first century. She is ritually connected to all American writers by her search for her own distinct voice, and she speaks of the human condition unbound by time or place.

Thus is Celia Thaxter's "Appledore Edition" of *Poems* reissued in 1996, a century after Sarah Orne Jewett so ably edited the poetry of her beloved friend.

## Bibliography of the Works of Celia Laighton Thaxter

*Poems.* New York: Hurd and Houghton, 1872, 1874, 1876.

*Among the Isles of Shoals.* Boston: J. R. Osgood & Co., 1873; Portsmouth, NH: Peter E. Randall Publisher, 1994

*Drift-Weed.* Boston: Houghton, Osgood & Co., 1879; Houghton Mifflin Co., 1894.

*Poems for Children.* Boston: Houghton Mifflin Co., 1883,

*The Cruise of the Mystery, and other Poems.* Boston: Houghton Mifflin Co., 1886.

*Idyls and Pastorals: A Home Gallery of Poetry and Art.* Boston: Lothrop & Co., 1886.

*Yule Log.* New York: Prang, 1889.

*My Lighthouse, and Other Poems.* Boston: Prang, 1890.

*Verses.* Boston: Lothrop, 1891.

*An Island Garden.* Boston: Houghton Mifflin Co., 1894, 1904, 1988; Bowie, Md.: Heritage Books, 1978; Ithaca, NY: Bulbriar Press, 1985.

*Stories and Poems for Children.* Boston: Houghton Mifflin Co., 1896, 1896, 1906.

*Letters of Celia Thaxter.* Edited by Annie Fields and Rose Lamb. Boston: Houghton Mifflin Co., 1896, 1897.

*The Poems of Celia Thaxter.* Edited by Annie Fields and Rose Lamb. Appledore Edition. Boston, Houghton Mifflin Co., 1896, 1899, 1902, 1906.

*The Heavenly Guest.* Edited by Oscar Laighton, Andover, Mass., Smith & Coutts, 1935.

*Sandpiper, and Sandalphon.* Taylorville, Ill., Parker Publishing Co., n.d.

*Maize, the Nation's Emblem.* Taylorville, Ill., Parker Publishing Co., n.d.

## Primary Source Materials of Celia Thaxter

Although some Thaxter materials are still in the hands of Thaxter family members and friends, many primary source materials such as letters, diaries, photographs, drawings, paintings, painted china, autograph books, and scrapbooks are available at the following libraries:

Boston Public Library, Boston, MA. Contains letters, sheet music of Thaxter's songs, and Annie Fields materials.

Dimond Library, University of New Hampshire, Durham, NH. Contains an excellent collection of Isles of Shoals photographs.

Houghton Library, Harvard University, Cambridge MA. See also the Schlesinger Library at Radcliffe College.

The Huntington Library. San Marino, CA. Thaxter materials are included in the James and Annie Fields Collection. A major source of letters.

Miller Library, Colby College, Waterville, ME. Rosamond Thaxter gave many of her materials to this well organized collection. Jewett materials can also be found here.

Portsmouth Athenaeum. Portsmouth, NH. Contains an Isles of Shoals Collection. See also the Portsmouth Public Library and the Thayer Cummings Library at Strawbery Banke in Portsmouth, NH.

Star Island Bookstore, Oceanic Hotel, Star Island, off Portsmouth, NH. Open only in summer. Sells a variety of books about Thaxter and the Isles of Shoals. A similar small bookstore is open on Appledore Island at the Shoals Marine Laboratory

Vaughn Cottage, Thaxter Room, Star Island, off Portsmouth, NH. Materials here are owned by the Star Island Corporation, and are accessible only during summer months on the island. Much valuable Isles of Shoals history as well as Thaxter memorabilia. Materials once in the hands of Barbara Durant, a Thaxter family member, have recently been deposited here.

Westbrook College, Portland, ME. Maine Women Writers' Collective. Contains primary materials on Thaxter and her circle. Also many first editions of their works.

Scholars should also investigate materials of Sarah Orne Jewett, James Fields, Annie Adams Fields, John Greenleaf Whittier, Thomas Wentworth Higginson, Childe Hassam, and other members of Celia Thaxter's circle. Books and articles by Jane E. Vallier contain a substantial amount of information on both primary and secondary sources relating to Thaxter.

## `Biographies of Celia Laighton Thaxter

Fields, Annie Adams. "Celia Thaxter," *Authors and Friends.*, Boston: Houghton Mifflin Company, 1897.

Labanaris, Faye. *Blossoms By The Sea*. Paducah, KY: American Quilter's Society, 1996.

Older, Julia. *The Island Queen: A Novel*. Hancock, NH: Appledore Books, 1994. A fictionalized version of the Thaxter story.

Thaxter, Rosamond. *Sandpiper: The Life and Letters of Celia Thaxter.* Portsmouth, NH: Peter Randall, 1982. Contains selected poems.

Vallier, Jane E. *Poet On Demand: The Life, Letters and Works of Celia Thaxter.* Camden, ME: Down East Books, 1982. Second edition, Portsmouth, NH: Peter E. Randall Publisher, 1994. Contains extensive bibliographies and selected poems.

## Selected Secondary Sources on Celia Thaxter

Blanchard, Paula. *Sarah Orne Jewett: Her World and Her Work*. Reading, MA: Addison-Wesley Publishing Company. Radcliffe Biography Series, 1994.

Curry, David Park. *Childe Hassam: An Island Garden Revisited* . New York: Norton, 1990.

Fetterley, Judith and Marjorie Pryse (eds.) *American Women Regionalists, 1850-1910.* New York: Norton, 1992.

Mason, Caleb. *The Isles of Shoals Remembered: A Legacy from America's First Musicians' and Artists' Colony.* Boston: Charles E. Tuttle and Company, 1992.

Norwood, Vera. *Made from this Earth: American Women and Nature*. Chapel Hill: North Carolina University Press, 1993.

Roman, Judith. *Annie Adams Fields: The Spirit of Charles Street.* Bloomington, IN: University of Indiana Press, 1990.

Shi, David E. *Facing Facts: Realism in American Thought and Culture, 1850-1920*. New York: Oxford University Press, 1995.

Springer, Haskell (ed.) *America and the Sea: A Literary History*. Athens, GA: University of Georgia Press, 1995.

Walker, Cheryl (ed.) *American Women Poets of the 19th Century : An Anthology*. New Brunswick, NJ: Rutgers University Press, 1992.

## A Bibliography of Celia Thaxter Lyrics Set to Music

Bonneau Gilles Yves. "Seaward," 1992.*

Burdett, G. A. "Dawn: A rush of wings in the dawn," Boston: Oliver Ditson and Co. 1880.

Clayton, John. "Because of Thee," Boston: Arthur P. Schmidt, 1890.

Cobb, Lila. "The Wild Rose" and "Foreboding," 1992.*

Dobrinski, Denis. "Song: The Summer Madrigal," 1992.*

Eichberg, Julius. "Sing Little Bird," "The Wild Rose," "Sunset Song" "Foreboding," and "O Swallow Sailing Lightly," Boston: Oliver Ditson and Co. Circa 1889.

Hall, Greg. "Foreboding," 1992.*

Hecker, Zeke. "Alone," 1992.*

Humez, Nick. "Three Thaxter Songs: "Wait," "Mutation," and "Sunset Song," 1992.*

Johns, Clayton. "Because of Thee," Boston: Arthur Schmidt and Co., 1886.

Kaufmann, Charles. "Two Thaxter Songs: Her Mirror, and "Song.," 1992.*

Lang, Margaret Ruthven. "I Wore Your Roses Yesterday," MS, 1891.

McDonald, John. "Three Thaxter Songs: Sing, Little Bird, The Wild Rose, and Sunset Song," 1992.*

McLean, Don. "From *Among the Isles of Shoals*," 1992.*

Paine, John Knowles. "Two Thaxter Songs: I Wore Your Roses Yesterday, and "A Bird Upon a Rosy Bough," circa 1880.

Rogers, Clara Kathleen. "The Answer," and "The Blossoms Blush on the Bough," Boston: Arthur P. Schmidt and Co., 1888.

Schlesinger, Sebastian B. "Slumber Song," " Thou Little Child with Tender Clinging Arms," (with violin obligato) , Boston: Arthur P. Schmidt and Co., 1886.

Vannah, Kate. "Good Bye, Sweet Day," Boston: Louis H. Ross and Co., 1891.

Viens, Michael. "Song: We Sail Toward Evening's Lonely Star," 1992.*

*Written for the Maine Composers' Forum Festival: "Celia Thaxter's Parlor Revisited," August 23, 1992, South Congregational Church Kennebunkport, ME. (Maine Composers' Forum, PO Box 8763, Portland, ME 04104.)

The Star Island Corporation has several Thaxter hymns such as "My Lighthouse," and "Love Shall Save Us All" printed in small conference song books at the Vaughn Library on Star Island. Other Thaxter lyrics have been sung to traditional hymn melodies.

# THE POEMS

OF

# CELIA THAXTER

BOSTON AND NEW YORK
HOUGHTON, MIFFLIN AND COMPANY
The Riverside Press, Cambridge
1896

*Sarah Orne Jewett*
*Courtesy University of New Hampshire*

IN this new edition of the collected writings of Celia Thaxter, great care has been taken to keep to her own arrangement and to the order in which the poems were originally published. In this way they seem to make something like a journal of her daily life and thought, and to mark the constantly increasing power of observation which was so marked a trait in her character. As her eyes grew quicker to see the blooming of flowers and the flight of birds, the turn of the waves as they broke on the rocks of Appledore, so the eyes of her spirit read more and more clearly the inward significance of things, the mysterious sorrows and joys of human life. In the earliest of her poems there is much to be found of that strange insight and anticipation of experience which comes with such gifts of nature and gifts for writing as hers, but as life went on it seemed as if Sorrow were visible to her eyes, a shrouded figure walking in the daylight. *Here I and Sorrow sit* was often true to the sad vision of her imagination, yet she oftenest came hand in hand with some invisible dancing Joy to a friend's door.

Through the long list of these brief poems (beginning in the earliest book with *Land-locked* and following through the volumes called *Driftweed* and *The Cruise of the Mystery* ; all reprinted here with some later verses found together among her papers), one walks side by side in intimate companionship with this sometimes sad-hearted but sincerely glad and happy woman and poet, and knows the springs of her life and the power of her great love and hope. In another volume all her delightful verses and stories for children have been gathered; but one poem, *The Sandpiper*, seemed to belong to one book as much as to the other, and this has been reprinted in both.

In the volume of her *Letters* will be found the records of Celia Thaxter's life and so far as it could be told the history of her literary work, while some personal notes by the hand of one of her dearest and oldest friends leave little to be said here. Yet those who have known through her writings alone the islands she loved so much, may care to know how, just before she died, she paid, as if with dim foreboding, a last visit to the old familiar places of the tiny world that was so dear to her. Day after day she called those who were with her to walk or sail; once to spend a long afternoon among the high cliffs of Star Island where we sat in the shade behind the old church, and she spoke of the year that she spent in the Gosport parsonage, and went there with us, to find old memories waiting to surprise her in the worn doorways, and ghosts and fancies of her youth tenanting all the an-

cient rooms.   Once we went to the lighthouse on
White Island, where she walked lightly over the
rough rocks with wonted feet, and showed us many
a trace of her childhood, and sang some quaint old
songs, as we sat on the cliff looking seaward, with
a touching lovely cadence in her voice, an unfor-
gotten cadence to any one who ever heard her sing.
We sat by the Spaniards' graves through a long
summer twilight, and she repeated her poem as if its
familiar words were new, and we talked of many
things as we watched the sea.   And on Appledore she
showed us all the childish playgrounds dearest to her
and to her brothers, — the cupboard in a crevice of
rock, the old wells and cellars, the tiny stone-walled
enclosures, the worn doorsteps of unremembered houses.
We crept under the Sheep rock for shelter out of a
sudden gust of rain, we found some of the rarer wild
flowers in their secret places.   In one of these it
thrills me now to remember that she saw a new white
flower, strange to her and to the island, which seemed
to reach up to her hand.   "This never bloomed on
Appledore before," she said, and looked at it with
grave wonder.   "It has not quite bloomed yet," she
said, standing before the flower; " I shall come here
again;" and then we went our unreturning way up the
footpath that led over the ledges, and left the new
flower growing in its deep windless hollow on the soft
green turf.

It was midsummer, and the bayberry bushes were all a bright and shining green, and we watched a sandpiper, and heard the plaintive cry that begged us not to find and trouble its nest. Under the very rocks and gray ledges, to the far nests of the wild sea birds, her love and knowledge seemed to go. She was made of that very dust, and set about with that sea, islanded indeed in the reserves of her lonely nature with its storms and calmness of high tides, but it seemed as if a little star dust must have been mixed with the ordinary dust of those coasts; there was something bright in her spirit that will forever shine, and light the hearts of those who loved her. It will pass on to a later time in these poems that she wrote of music, of spring and winter, of flowers and birds, and of that northern sea which was her friend and fellow.

S. O. J.

# CONTENTS

1 By Oscar Laighton.

# CONTENTS

# POEMS

## LAND-LOCKED

BLACK lie the hills; swiftly doth daylight flee;
    And, catching gleams of sunset's dying smile,
    Through the dusk land for many a changing mile
The river runneth softly to the sea.

O happy river, could I follow thee!
    O yearning heart, that never can be still!
    O wistful eyes, that watch the steadfast hill,
Longing for level line of solemn sea!

Have patience; here are flowers and songs of birds,
    Beauty and fragrance, wealth of sound and sight,
    All summer's glory thine from morn till night,
And life too full of joy for uttered words.

Neither am I ungrateful; but I dream
    Deliciously how twilight falls to-night
    Over the glimmering water, how the light
Dies blissfully away, until I seem

To feel the wind, sea-scented, on my cheek,
　To catch the sound of dusky flapping sail
　And dip of oars, and voices on the gale
Afar off, calling low, — my name they speak!

O Earth! thy summer song of joy may soar
　Ringing to heaven in triumph.　I but crave
　The sad, caressing murmur of the wave
That breaks in tender music on the shore.


## OFF  SHORE

Rock, little boat, beneath the quiet sky;
Only the stars behold us where we lie, —
Only the stars and yonder brightening moon.

On the wide sea to-night alone are we;
The sweet, bright summer day dies silently,
Its glowing sunset will have faded soon.

Rock softly, little boat, the while I mark
The far off gliding sails, distinct and dark,
Across the west pass steadily and slow.

But on the eastern waters sad, they change
And vanish, dream-like, gray, and cold, and strange,
And no one knoweth whither they may go.

We care not, we, drifting with wind and tide,
While glad waves darken upon either side,
Save where the moon sends silver sparkles down,

And yonder slender stream of changing light,
Now white, now crimson, tremulously bright,
Where dark the lighthouse stands, with fiery crown.

Thick falls the dew, soundless on sea and shore:
It shines on little boat and idle oar,
Wherever moonbeams touch with tranquil glow.

The waves are full of whispers wild and sweet;
They call to me, — incessantly they beat
Along the boat from stern to curvèd prow.

Comes the careering wind, blows back my hair,
All damp with dew, to kiss me unaware,
Murmuring "Thee I love," and passes on.

Sweet sounds on rocky shores the distant rote;
Oh could we float forever, little boat,
Under the blissful sky drifting alone!

## EXPECTATION

THROUGHOUT the lonely house the whole day long
  The wind-harp's fitful music sinks and swells, —
A cry of pain, sometimes, or sad and strong,
  Or faint, like broken peals of silver bells.

Across the little garden comes the breeze,
  Bows all its cups of flame, and brings to me
Its breath of mignonette and bright sweet-peas,
  With drowsy murmurs from the encircling sea.

In at the open door a crimson drift
  Of fluttering, fading woodbine leaves is blown,
And through the clambering vine the sunbeams sift,
  And trembling shadows on the floor are thrown.

I climb the stair, and from the window lean
  Seeking thy sail, O love, that still delays;
Longing to catch its glimmer, searching keen
  The jealous distance veiled in tender haze.

What care I if the pansies purple be,
  Or sweet the wind-harp wails through the slow
      hours;
Or that the lulling music of the sea
  Comes woven with the perfume of the flowers?

Thou comest not!  I ponder o'er the leaves,
  The crimson drift behind the open door:
Soon shall we listen to a wind that grieves,
  Mourning this glad year, dead forevermore.

And, O my love, shall we on some sad day
  Find joys and hopes low fallen like the leaves,
Blown by life's chilly autumn wind away
  In withered heaps God's eye alone perceives?

Come thou, and save me from my dreary thought!
  Who dares to question Time, what it may bring?
Yet round us lies the radiant summer, fraught
  With beauty: must we dream of suffering?

Yea, even so.  Through this enchanted land,
  This morning-red of life, we go to meet
The tempest in the desert, hand in hand,
  Along God's paths of pain, that seek his feet.

But this one golden moment, — hold it fast!
  The light grows long: low in the west the sun,
Clear red and glorious, slowly sinks at last,
  And while I muse, the tranquil day is done.

The land breeze freshens in thy gleaming sail!
  Across the singing waves the shadows creep:
Under the new moon's thread of silver pale,
  With the first star, thou comest o'er the deep.

## THE WRECK OF THE POCAHONTAS

I LIT the lamps in the lighthouse tower,
  For the sun dropped down and the day was dead.
They shone like a glorious clustered flower, —
  Ten golden and five red.

Looking across, where the line of coast
  Stretched darkly, shrinking away from the sea,
The lights sprang out at its edge, — almost
  They seemed to answer me!

O warning lights! burn bright and clear,
  Hither the storm comes!　Leagues away
It moans and thunders low and drear, —
  Burn till the break of day!

Good-night! I called to the gulls that sailed
  Slow past me through the evening sky;
And my comrades, answering shrilly, hailed
  Me back with boding cry.

A mournful breeze began to blow;
  Weird music it drew through the iron bars;
The sullen billows boiled below,
  And dimly peered the stars;

The sails that flecked the ocean floor
 From east to west leaned low and fled;
They knew what came in the distant roar
 That filled the air with dread!

Flung by a fitful gust, there beat
 Against the window a dash of rain:
Steady as tramp of marching feet
 Strode on the hurricane.

It smote the waves for a moment still,
 Level and deadly white for fear;
The bare rock shuddered, — an awful thrill
 Shook even my tower of cheer.

Like all the demons loosed at last,
 Whistling and shrieking, wild and wide,
The mad wind raged, while strong and fast
 Rolled in the rising tide.

And soon in ponderous showers, the spray,
 Struck from the granite, reared and sprung
And clutched at tower and cottage gray,
 Where overwhelmed they clung

Half drowning to the naked rock;
 But still burned on the faithful light,
Nor faltered at the tempest's shock,
 Through all the fearful night.

Was it in vain? That knew not we.
    We seemed, in that confusion vast
Of rushing wind and roaring sea,
    One point whereon was cast

The whole Atlantic's weight of brine.
    Heaven help the ship should drift our way!
No matter how the light might shine
    Far on into the day.

When morning dawned, above the din
    Of gale and breaker boomed a gun!
Another! We who sat within
    Answered with cries each one.*

Into each other's eyes with fear
    We looked through helpless tears, as still,
One after one, near and more near,
    The signals pealed, until

The thick storm seemed to break apart
    To show us, staggering to her grave,
The fated brig. We had no heart
    To look, for naught could save.

One glimpse of black hull heaving slow,
    Then closed the mists o'er canvas torn
And tangled ropes swept to and fro
    From masts that raked forlorn.

Weeks after, yet ringed round with spray
　　Our island lay, and none might land;
Though blue the waters of the bay
　　Stretched calm on either hand.

And when at last from the distant shore
　　A little boat stole out, to reach
Our loneliness, and bring once more
　　Fresh human thought and speech,

We told our tale, and the boatmen cried:
　　"'T was the Pocahontas, — all were lost!
For miles along the coast the tide
　　Her shattered timbers tossed."

Then I looked the whole horizon round, —
　　So beautiful the ocean spread
About us, o'er those sailors drowned!
　　"Father in heaven," I said, —

A child's grief struggling in my breast, —
　　"Do purposeless thy children meet
Such bitter death?　How was it best
　　These hearts should cease to beat?

"Oh wherefore?　Are we naught to Thee?
　　Like senseless weeds that rise and fall
Upon thine awful sea, are we
　　No more then, after all?"

And I shut the beauty from my sight,
   For I thought of the dead that lay below;
From the bright air faded the warmth and light,
   There came a chill like snow.

Then I heard the far-off rote resound,
   Where the breakers slow and slumberous rolled,
And a subtile sense of Thought profound
   Touched me with power untold.

And like a voice eternal spake
   That wondrous rhythm, and, "Peace, be still!"
It murmured, "bow thy head and take
   Life's rapture and life's ill,

"And wait.   At last all shall be clear."
   The long, low, mellow music rose
And fell, and soothed my dreaming ear
   With infinite repose.

Sighing I climbed the lighthouse stair,
   Half forgetting my grief and pain;
And while the day died, sweet and fair,
   I lit the lamps again.

## A THANKSGIVING

HIGH on the ledge the wind blows the bayberry
    bright,
Turning the leaves till they shudder and shine in the
    light;
Yellow St. John's-wort and yarrow are nodding their
    heads,
Iris and wild-rose are glowing in purples and reds.

Swift flies the schooner careering beyond o'er the blue;
Faint shows the furrow she leaves as she cleaves lightly
    through;
Gay gleams the fluttering flag at her delicate mast;
Full swell the sails with the wind that is following fast.

Quail and sandpiper and swallow and sparrow are here:
Sweet sound their manifold notes, high and low, far
    and near;
Chorus of musical waters, the rush of the breeze,
Steady and strong from the south, — what glad voices
    are these!

O cup of the wild-rose, curved close to hold odorous
    dew,
What thought do you hide in your heart? I would
    that I knew!

O beautiful Iris, unfurling your purple and gold,
What victory fling you abroad in the flags you unfold?

Sweet may your thought be, red rose, but still sweeter
      is mine,
Close in my heart hidden, clear as your dewdrop
      divine.
Flutter your gonfalons, Iris, the pæan I sing
Is for victory better than joy or than beauty can bring.

Into thy calm eyes, O Nature, I look and rejoice;
Prayerful, I add my one note to the Infinite voice:
As shining and singing and sparkling glides on the
      glad day,
And eastward the swift-rolling planet wheels into the
      gray.

## THE MINUTE–GUNS

I STOOD within the little cove,
    Full of the morning's life and hope,
While heavily the eager waves
    Charged thundering up the rocky slope.

The splendid breakers! How they rushed,
    All emerald green and flashing white,
Tumultuous in the morning sun,
    With cheer and sparkle and delight!

And freshly blew the fragrant wind,
  The wild sea wind, across their tops,
And caught the spray and flung it far
  In sweeping showers of glittering drops.

Within the cove all flashed and foamed
  With many a fleeting rainbow hue;
Without, gleamed bright against the sky
  A tender wavering line of blue,

Where tossed the distant waves, and far
  Shone silver-white a quiet sail;
And overhead the soaring gulls
  With graceful pinions stemmed the gale.

And all my pulses thrilled with joy,
  Watching the winds' and waters' strife,
With sudden rapture, — and I cried,
  "Oh, sweet is life!  Thank God for life!"

Sailed any cloud across the sky,
  Marring this glory of the sun's?
Over the sea, from distant forts,
  There came the boom of minute-guns!

War-tidings!  Many a brave soul fled,
  And many a heart the message stuns!
I saw no more the joyous waves,
  I only heard the minute-guns.

## SEAWARD

TO ——

How long it seems since that mild April night,
  When, leaning from the window, you and I
Heard, clearly ringing from the shadowy bight,
  The loon's unearthly cry!

Southwest the wind blew, million little waves
  Ran rippling round the point in mellow tune,
But mournful, like the voice of one who raves,
  That laughter of the loon!

We called to him, while blindly through the haze
  Uprose the meagre moon behind us, slow,
So dim, the fleet of boats we scarce could trace,
  Moored lightly just below.

We called, and lo, he answered!   Half in fear
  We sent the note back.   Echoing rock and bay
Made melancholy music far and near,
  Sadly it died away.

That schooner, you remember?   Flying ghost!
  Her canvas catching every wandering beam,
Aerial, noiseless, past the glimmering coast
  She glided like a dream.

Would we were leaning from your window now,
　　Together calling to the eerie loon,
The fresh wind blowing care from either brow,
　　This sumptuous night of June!

So many sighs load this sweet inland air,
　　'T is hard to breathe, nor can we find relief, —
However lightly touched we all must share
　　This nobleness of grief.

But sighs are spent before they reach your ear;
　　Vaguely they mingle with the water's rune,
No sadder sound salutes you than the clear,
　　Wild laughter of the loon.


## ROCK WEEDS

So bleak these shores, wind-swept and all the year
　　Washed by the wild Atlantic's restless tide,
You would not dream that flowers the woods hold dear
　　Amid such desolation dare abide.

Yet when the bitter winter breaks, some day,
　　With soft winds fluttering her garments' hem,
Up from the sweet South comes the lingering May,
　　Sets the first wind-flower trembling on its stem;

Scatters her violets with lavish hands,
    White, blue, and amber; calls the columbine,
Till like clear flame in lonely nooks, gay bands
    Swinging their scarlet bells, obey the sign;

Makes buttercups and dandelions blaze,
    And throws in glimmering patches here and there,
The little eyebright's pearls, and gently lays
    The impress of her beauty everywhere.

Later, June bids the sweet wild rose to blow;
    Wakes from its dream the drowsy pimpernel;
Unfolds the bindweed's ivory buds, that glow
    As delicately blushing as a shell.

Then purple Iris smiles, and hour by hour,
    The fair procession multiplies; and soon,
In clusters creamy white, the elder-flower
    Waves its broad disk against the rising moon.

O'er quiet beaches shelving to the sea
    Tall mulleins sway, and thistles; all day long
Flows in the wooing water dreamily,
    With subtile music in its slumberous song.

Herb-robert hears, and princess'-feather bright,
    And goldthread clasps the little skull-cap blue;

And troops of swallows, gathering for their flight,
O'er goldenrod and asters hold review.

The barren island dreams in flowers, while blow
The south winds, drawing haze o'er sea and land;
Yet the great heart of ocean, throbbing slow,
Makes the frail blossoms vibrate where they stand;

And hints of heavier pulses soon to shake
Its mighty breast when summer is no more,
And devastating waves sweep on and break,
And clasp with girdle white the iron shore.

Close folded, safe within the sheltering seed,
Blossom and bell and leafy beauty hide;
Nor icy blast, nor bitter spray they heed,
But patiently their wondrous change abide.

The heart of God through his creation stirs,
We thrill to feel it, trembling as the flowers
That die to live again, — his messengers,
To keep faith firm in these sad souls of ours.

The waves of Time may devastate our lives,
The frosts of age may check our failing breath,
They shall not touch the spirit that survives
Triumphant over doubt and pain and death.

## THE SANDPIPER

Across the narrow beach we flit,
  One little sandpiper and I,
And fast I gather, bit by bit,
  The scattered driftwood bleached and dry.
The wild waves reach their hands for it,
  The wild wind raves, the tide runs high,
As up and down the beach we flit, —
  One little sandpiper and I.

Above our heads the sullen clouds
  Scud black and swift across the sky;
Like silent ghosts in misty shrouds
  Stand out the white lighthouses high.
Almost as far as eye can reach
  I see the close-reefed vessels fly,
As fast we flit along the beach, —
  One little sandpiper and I.

I watch him as he skims along,
  Uttering his sweet and mournful cry.
He starts not at my fitful song,
  Or flash of fluttering drapery.
He has no thought of any wrong;
  He scans me with a fearless eye.
Stanch friends are we, well tried and strong,
  The little sandpiper and I.

Comrade, where wilt thou be to-night
    When the loosed storm breaks furiously?
My driftwood fire will burn so bright!
    To what warm shelter canst thou fly?
I do not fear for thee, though wroth
    The tempest rushes through the sky:
For are we not God's children both,
    Thou, little sandpiper, and I?

## TWILIGHT

SEPTEMBER'S slender crescent grows again
    Distinct in yonder peaceful evening red,
    Clearer the stars are sparkling overhead,
And all the sky is pure, without a stain.

Cool blows the evening wind from out the West
    And bows the flowers, the last sweet flowers that
        bloom, —
    Pale asters, many a heavy-waving plume
Of goldenrod that bends as if opprest.

The summer's songs are hushed.   Up the lone shore
    The weary waves wash sadly, and a grief
    Sounds in the wind, like farewells fond and brief.
The cricket's chirp but makes the silence more.

Life's autumn comes; the leaves begin to fall;
   The moods of spring and summer pass away;
   The glory and the rapture, day by day,
Depart, and soon the quiet grave folds all.

O thoughtful sky, how many eyes in vain
   Are lifted to your beauty, full of tears!
   How many hearts go back through all the years,
Heavy with loss, eager with questioning pain,

To read the dim Hereafter, to obtain
   One glimpse beyond the earthly curtain, where
   Their dearest dwell, where they may be or e'er
September's slender crescent shines again!

## THE SWALLOW

THE swallow twitters about the eaves;
   Blithely she sings, and sweet and clear;
Around her climb the woodbine leaves
   In a golden atmosphere.

The summer wind sways leaf and spray,
   That catch and cling to the cool gray wall;
The bright sea stretches miles away,
   And the noon sun shines o'er all.

In the chamber's shadow, quietly,
  I stand and worship the sky and the leaves,
The golden air and the brilliant sea,
  The swallow at the eaves.

Like a living jewel she sits and sings;
  Fain would I read her riddle aright,
Fain would I know whence her rapture springs,
  So strong in a thing so slight!

The fine, clear fire of joy that steals
  Through all my spirit at what I see
In the glimpse my window's space reveals, —
  That seems no mystery!

But scarce for her joy can she utter her song;
  Yet she knows not the beauty of skies or seas.
Is it bliss of living, so sweet and strong?
  Is it love, which is more than these?

O happy creature! what stirs thee so?
  A spark of the gladness of God thou art.
Why should we seek to find and to know
  The secret of thy heart?

Before the gates of his mystery
  Trembling we knock with an eager hand;
Silent behind them waiteth He;
  Not yet may we understand.

But thrilling throughout the universe
  Throbs the pulse of his mighty will,
Till we gain the knowledge of joy or curse
  In the choice of good or ill.

He looks from the eyes of the little child,
  And searches souls with their gaze so clear;
To the heart some agony makes wild
  He whispers, "I am here."

He smiles in the face of every flower;
  In the swallow's twitter of sweet content
He speaks, and we follow through every hour
  The way his deep thought went.

Here should be courage and hope and faith;
  Naught has escaped the trace of his hand;
And a voice in the heart of his silence saith,
  One day we shall understand.


## A GRATEFUL HEART

LAST night I stole away alone, to find
  A mellow crescent setting o'er the sea,
  And lingered in its light, while over me
Blew fitfully the grieving autumn wind.

And somewhat sadly to myself I said,
  "Summer is gone," and watched how bright and
      fast
  Through the moon's track the little waves sped
      past, —
"Summer is gone! her golden days are dead."

Regretfully I thought, "Since I have trod
  Earth's ways with willing or reluctant feet,
  Never did season bring me days more sweet,
Crowned with rare joys and priceless gifts from God.

"And they are gone: they will return no more."
  The slender moon went down, all red and still:
  The stars shone clear, the silent dews fell chill;
The waves with ceaseless murmur washed the shore.

A low voice spake: "And wherefore art thou sad?
  Here in thy heart all summer folded lies,
  And smiles in sunshine though the sweet time dies:
'T is thine to keep forever fresh and glad!"

Yea, gentle voice, though the fair days depart,
  And skies grow cold above the restless sea,
  God's gifts are measureless, and there shall be
Eternal summer in the grateful heart.

## THE SPANIARDS' GRAVES

### AT THE ISLES OF SHOALS

O SAILORS, did sweet eyes look after you
   The day you sailed away from sunny Spain?
Bright eyes that followed fading ship and crew,
   Melting in tender rain?

Did no one dream of that drear night to be,
   Wild with the wind, fierce with the stinging snow,
When on yon granite point that frets the sea,
   The ship met her death-blow?

Fifty long years ago these sailors died:
   (None know how many sleep beneath the waves:)
Fourteen gray headstones, rising side by side,
   Point out their nameless graves, —

Lonely, unknown, deserted, but for me,
   And the wild birds that flit with mournful cry,
And sadder winds, and voices of the sea
   That moans perpetually.

Wives, mothers, maidens, wistfully, in vain
   Questioned the distance for the yearning sail,
That, leaning landward, should have stretched again
   White arms wide on the gale,

To bring back their beloved.    Year by year,
   Weary they watched, till youth and beauty passed,
And lustrous eyes grew dim and age drew near,
   And hope was dead at last.

Still summer broods o'er that delicious land,
   Rich, fragrant, warm with skies of golden glow:
Live any yet of that forsaken band
   Who loved so long ago?

O Spanish women, over the far seas,
   Could I but show you where your dead repose!
Could I send tidings on this northern breeze
   That strong and steady blows!

Dear dark-eyed sisters, you remember yet
   These you have lost, but you can never know
One stands at their bleak graves whose eyes are
      wet
   With thinking of your woe!

## WATCHING

In childhood's season fair,
On many a balmy, moonless summer night,
While wheeled the lighthouse arms of dark and bright
   Far through the humid air;

How patient have I been,
Sitting alone, a happy little maid,
Waiting to see, careless and unafraid,
    My father's boat come in;

Close to the water's edge
Holding a tiny spark, that he might steer
(So dangerous the landing, far and near)
    Safe past the ragged ledge.

I had no fears, — not one;
The wild, wide waste of water leagues around
Washed ceaselessly; there was no human sound,
    And I was all alone.

But Nature was so kind!
Like a dear friend I loved the loneliness;
My heart rose glad, as at some sweet caress,
    When passed the wandering wind.

Yet it was joy to hear,
From out the darkness, sounds grow clear at last,
Of rattling rowlock, and of creaking mast,
    And voices drawing near!

"Is 't thou, dear father?   Say!"
What well-known shout resounded in reply,
As loomed the tall sail, smitten suddenly
    With the great lighthouse ray!

I will be patient now,
Dear Heavenly Father, waiting here for Thee:
I know the darkness holds Thee.   Shall I be
   Afraid, when it is Thou?

On thy eternal shore,
In pauses, when life's tide is at its prime,
I hear the everlasting rote of Time
   Beating for evermore.

Shall I not then rejoice?
Oh, never lost or sad should child of thine
Sit waiting, fearing lest there come no sign,
   No whisper of thy voice!

## IN MAY

THAT was a curlew calling overhead,
   That fine, clear whistle shaken from the clouds:
See! hovering o'er the swamp with wings outspread,
   He sinks where at its edge in shining crowds
The yellow violets dance as they unfold,
In the blithe spring wind, all their green and gold.

Blithe south-wind, spreading bloom upon the sea,
   Drawing about the world this band of haze
So softly delicate, and bringing me
   A touch of balm that like a blessing stays;

Though beauty like a dream bathes sea and land,
For the first time Death holds me by the hand.

Yet none the less the swallows weave above
   Through the bright air a web of light and song,
And calling clear and sweet from cove to cove,
   The sandpiper, the lonely rocks among,
Makes wistful music, and the singing sea
Sends its strong chorus upward solemnly.

O Mother Nature, infinitely dear!
   Vainly I search the beauty of thy face,
Vainly thy myriad voices charm my ear;
   I cannot gather from thee any trace
Of God's intent.    Help me to understand
Why, this sweet morn, Death holds me by the hand.

I watch the waves, shoulder to shoulder set,
   That strive and vanish and are seen no more.
The earth is sown with graves that we forget,
   And races of mankind the wide world o'er
Rise, strive, and vanish, leaving naught behind,
Like changing waves swept by the changing wind.

"Hard-hearted, cold, and blind," she answers me,
   "Vexing thy soul with riddles hard to guess!
No waste of any atom canst thou see,
   Nor make I any gesture purposeless.

Lift thy dim eyes up to the conscious sky!
God *meant* that rapture in the curlew's cry.

"He holds his whirling worlds in check; not one
    May from its awful orbit swerve aside;
Yet breathes He in this south-wind, bids the sun
    Wake the fair flowers He fashioned, far and wide,
And this strong pain thou canst not understand
Is but his grasp on thy reluctant hand."

## A SUMMER DAY

At daybreak in the fresh light, joyfully
    The fishermen drew in their laden net;
The shore shone rosy purple, and the sea
    Was streaked with violet;

And pink with sunrise, many a shadowy sail
    Lay southward, lighting up the sleeping bay;
And in the west the white moon, still and pale,
    Faded before the day.

Silence was everywhere.  The rising tide
    Slowly filled every cove and inlet small;
A musical low whisper, multiplied,
    You heard, and that was all.

No clouds at dawn, but as the sun climbed higher,
    White columns, thunderous, splendid, up the sky

Floated and stood, heaped in his steady fire,
    A stately company.

Stealing along the coast from cape to cape
    The weird mirage crept tremulously on,
In many a magic change and wondrous shape,
    Throbbing beneath the sun.

At noon the wind rose, swept the glassy sea
    To sudden ripple, thrust against the clouds
A strenuous shoulder, gathering steadily,
    Drove them before in crowds;

Till all the west was dark, and inky black
    The level-ruffled water underneath,
And up the wind cloud tossed, — a ghostly rack,
    In many a ragged wreath.

Then sudden roared the thunder, a great peal
    Magnificent, that broke and rolled away;
And down the wind plunged, like a furious keel,
    Cleaving the sea to spray;

And brought the rain sweeping o'er land and sea.
    And then was tumult!  Lightning sharp and
        keen,
Thunder, wind, rain, — a mighty jubilee
    The heaven and earth between!

Loud the roused ocean sang, a chorus grand;
   A solemn music rolled in undertone
Of waves that broke about, on either hand,
     The little island lone;

Where, joyful in his tempest as his calm,
   Held in the hollow of that hand of his,
I joined with heart and soul in God's great psalm,
     Thrilled with a nameless bliss.

Soon lulled the wind, the summer storm soon died;
   The shattered clouds went eastward, drifting slow;
From the low sun the rain-fringe swept aside,
     Bright in his rosy glow,

And wide a splendor streamed through all the sky;
   O'er sea and land one soft, delicious blush,
That touched the gray rocks lightly, tenderly;
     A transitory flush.

Warm, odorous gusts blew off the distant land,
   With spice of pine-woods, breath of hay new
      mown,
O'er miles of waves and sea scents cool and bland,
     Full in our faces blown.

Slow faded the sweet light, and peacefully
   The quiet stars came out, one after one:

The holy twilight fell upon the sea,
　　The summer day was done.

Such unalloyed delight its hours had given,
　　Musing, this thought rose in my grateful mind,
That God, who watches all things, up in heaven,
　　With patient eyes and kind,

Saw and was pleased, perhaps, one child of his
　　Dared to be happy like the little birds,
Because He gave his children days like this,
　　Rejoicing beyond words;

Dared, lifting up to Him untroubled eyes
　　In gratitude that worship is, and prayer,
Sing and be glad with ever new surprise,
　　He made his world so fair!


## REGRET

SOFTLY Death touched her, and she passed away
　　Out of this glad, bright world she made more fair,
Sweet as the apple-blossoms, when in May
　　The orchards flush, of summer grown aware.

All that fresh, delicate beauty gone from sight,
　　That gentle, gracious presence felt no more!
How must the house be emptied of delight,
　　What shadows on the threshold she passed o'er!

She loved me.   Surely I was grateful, yet
  I could not give her back all she gave me.
Ever I think of it with vague regret,
  Musing upon a summer by the sea:

Remembering troops of merry girls who pressed
  About me — clinging arms and tender eyes,
And love, like scent of roses.   With the rest
  She came, to fill my heart with new surprise.

The day I left them all, and sailed away,
  While o'er the calm sea, 'neath the soft gray sky,
They waved farewell, she followed me, to say
  Yet once again her wistful, sweet "good-by."

At the boat's bow she drooped; her light-green dress
  Swept o'er the skiff in many a graceful fold;
Her glowing face, bright with a mute caress,
  Crowned with her lovely hair of shadowy gold:

And tears she dropped into the crystal brine
  For me, unworthy — as we slowly swung
Free of the mooring.   Her last look was mine,
  Seeking me still the motley crowd among.

O tender memory of the dead I hold
  So precious through the fret and change of years!
Were I to live till Time itself grew old,
  The sad sea would be sadder for those tears.

## BEFORE SUNRISE

THIS grassy gorge, as daylight failed last night,
　I traversed toward the west, where, thin and
　　young,
Bent like Diana's bow and silver bright,
　Half lost in rosy haze, a crescent hung.

I paused upon the beach's upper edge:
　The violet east all shadowy lay behind;
Southward the lighthouse glittered o'er the ledge,
　And lightly, softly blew the western wind.

And at my feet, between the turf and stone,
　Wild roses, bayberry, purple thistles tall,
And pink herb-robert grew, where shells were strown
　And morning-glory vines climbed over all.

I stooped the closely folded buds to note,
　That gleamed in the dim light mysteriously,
While, full of whispers of the far-off rote,
　Summer's enchanted dusk crept o'er the sea.

And sights and sounds and sea-scents delicate,
　So wrought upon my soul with sense of bliss,
Happy I sat as if at heaven's gate,
　Asking on earth no greater joy than this.

And now, at dawn, upon the beach again,
  Kneeling I wait the coming of the sun,
Watching the looser-folded buds, and fain
  To see the marvel of their day begun.

All the world lies so dewy-fresh and still!
  Whispers so gently all the water wide,
Hardly it breaks the silence: from the hill
  Come clear bird-voices mingling with the tide.

Sunset or dawn: which is the lovelier? Lo!
  My darlings, sung to all the balmy night
By summer waves and softest winds that blow,
  Begin to feel the thrilling of the light!

Red lips of roses, waiting to be kissed
  By early sunshine, soon in smiles will break.
But oh, ye morning-glories, that keep tryst
  With the first ray of daybreak, ye awake!

O bells of triumph, ringing noiseless peals
  Of unimagined music to the day!
Almost I could believe each blossom feels
  The same delight that sweeps my soul away.

O bells of triumph! delicate trumpets, thrown
  Heavenward and earthward, turned east, west, north,
      south,

In lavish beauty, who through you has blown
  This sweet cheer of the morning with calm mouth?

'T is God who breathes the triumph; He who
      wrought
The tender curves, and laid the tints divine
Along the lovely lines; the Eternal Thought
  That troubles all our lives with wise design.

Yea, out of pain and death his beauty springs,
  And out of doubt a deathless confidence:
Though we are shod with leaden cares, our wings
  Shall lift us yet out of our deep suspense!

Thou great Creator!   Pardon us who reach
  For other heaven beyond this world of thine,
This matchless world, where thy least touch doth
      teach
  Thy solemn lessons clearly, line on line.

And help us to be grateful, we who live
  Such sordid, fretful lives of discontent,
Nor see the sunshine nor the flower, nor strive
  To find the love thy bitter chastening meant.

## BY THE ROADSIDE

DROPPED the warm rain from the brooding sky
    Softly all the summer afternoon;
Up the road I loitered carelessly,
    Glad to be alive in blissful June.

Though so gray the sky, and though the mist
    Swept the hills and half their beauty hid;
Though the scattering drops the broad leaves kissed,
    And no ray betwixt the vapor slid,

Yet the daisies tossed their white and gold
    In the quiet fields on either side,
And the green gloom deepened in the old
    Walnut-trees that flung their branches wide;

And the placid river wound away
    Westward to the hills through meadows fair,
Flower-fringed and starred, while blithe and gay
    Called the blackbirds through the balmy air.

Right and left I scanned the landscape round;
    Every shape, and scent, and wild bird's call,
Every color, curve, and gentle sound,
    Deep into my heart I gathered all.

Up I looked, and down upon the sod
  Sprinkled thick with violets blue and bright;
"Surely, 'Through his garden walketh God,'"
  Low I whispered, full of my delight.

Like a vision, on the path before,
  Came a little rosy, sun-browned maid,
Straying toward me from her cottage door,
  Paused, up-looking shyly, half afraid.

Never word she spake, but gazing so,
  Slow a smile rose to her clear brown eyes,
Overflowed her face with such a glow
  That I thrilled with sudden, sweet surprise.

Here was sunshine 'neath the cloudy skies!
  Low I knelt to bring her face to mine;
Sweeter, brighter grew her shining eyes,
  Yet she gave me neither word nor sign.

But within her look a blessing beamed;
  Meek I grew before it; was it just?
Was I worthy this pure light that streamed?
  Such approval, and such love and trust!

Half the flowers I carried in my hands
  Lightly in her pretty arms I laid:

Silent, but as one who understands,
  Clasped them close the rosy little maid.

Fair behind the honeysuckle spray
  Shone her innocent, delightful face!
Then I rose and slowly went my way,
  Left her standing, lighting all the place.

While her golden look stole after me,
  Lovelier bloomed the violets where I trod;
More divine earth's beauty seemed to be:
  "Through his garden visibly walked God."


## SORROW

UPON my lips she laid her touch divine,
  And merry speech and careless laughter died;
She fixed her melancholy eyes on mine,
  And would not be denied.

I saw the west wind loose his cloudlets white
  In flocks, careering through the April sky;
I could not sing though joy was at its height,
  For she stood silent by.

I watched the lovely evening fade away;
  A mist was lightly drawn across the stars;

She broke my quiet dream, I heard her say,
　"Behold your prison bars!

"Earth's gladness shall not satisfy your soul,
　　This beauty of the world in which you live;
The crowning grace that sanctifies the whole,
　　That, I alone can give."

I heard and shrank away from her afraid;
　　But still she held me and would still abide;
Youth's bounding pulses slackened and obeyed,
　　With slowly ebbing tide.

"Look thou beyond the evening star," she said,
　　"Beyond the changing splendors of the day;
Accept the pain, the weariness, the dread,
　　Accept and bid me stay!"

I turned and clasped her close with sudden strength,
　　And slowly, sweetly, I became aware
Within my arms God's angel stood at length,
　　White-robed and calm and fair.

And now I look beyond the evening star,
　　Beyond the changing splendors of the day,
Knowing the pain He sends more precious far,
　　More beautiful, than they.

## NOVEMBER

THERE is no wind at all to-night
　To dash the drops against the pane;
No sound abroad, nor any light,
　And sadly falls the autumn rain;

There is no color in the world,
　No lovely tint on hill or plain;
The summer's golden sails are furled,
　And sadly falls the autumn rain.

The earth lies tacitly beneath,
　As it were dead to joy or pain:
It does not move, it does not breathe, —
　And sadly falls the autumn rain.

And all my heart is patient too,
　I wait till it shall wake again;
The songs of spring shall sound anew,
　Though sadly falls the autumn rain.

## COURAGE

BECAUSE I hold it sinful to despond,
　And will not let the bitterness of life
Blind me with burning tears, but look beyond
　Its tumult and its strife;

Because I lift my head above the mist,
　　Where the sun shines and the broad breezes blow,
By every ray and every raindrop kissed
　　That God's love doth bestow;

Think you I find no bitterness at all?
　　No burden to be borne, like Christian's pack?
Think you there are no ready tears to fall
　　Because I keep them back?

Why should I hug life's ills with cold reserve,
　　To curse myself and all who love me?   Nay!
A thousand times more good than I deserve
　　God gives me every day.

And in each one of these rebellious tears,
　　Kept bravely back, He makes a rainbow shine;
Grateful I take his slightest gift, no fears
　　Nor any doubts are mine.

Dark skies must clear, and when the clouds are past,
　　One golden day redeems a weary year;
Patient I listen, sure that sweet at last
　　Will sound his voice of cheer.

Then vex me not with chiding.   Let me be.
　　I must be glad and grateful to the end.
I grudge you not your cold and darkness, — me
　　The powers of light befriend.

## REMEMBRANCE

FRAGRANT and soft the summer wind doth blow.
  Weary I lie, with heavy, half-shut eyes,
  And watch, while wistful thoughts within me
    rise,
The curtain idly swaying to and fro.

There comes a sound of household toil from far,
  A woven murmur: voices shrill and sweet,
  Clapping of doors, and restless moving feet,
And tokens faint of fret, and noise, and jar.

Without, the broad earth shimmers in the glare,
  Through the clear noon high rides the blazing
    sun,
  The birds are hushed; the cricket's chirp alone
With tremulous music cleaves the drowsy air.

I think, — "Past the gray rocks the wavelets run;
  The gold-brown seaweed drapes the ragged ledge;
  And brooding, silent, at the water's edge
The white gull sitteth, shining in the sun."

## SONG

WE sail toward evening's lonely star
　　That trembles in the tender blue;
One single cloud, a dusky bar,
　　Burnt with dull carmine through and through,
Slow smouldering in the summer sky,
　　Lies low along the fading west.
How sweet to watch its splendors die,
　　Wave-cradled thus and wind-earessed!

The soft breeze freshens, leaps the spray
　　To kiss our cheeks, with sudden cheer;
Upon the dark edge of the bay
　　Lighthouses kindle, far and near,
And through the warm deeps of the sky
　　Steal faint star-clusters, while we rest
In deep refreshment, thou and I,
　　Wave-cradled thus and wind-caressed.

How like a dream are earth and heaven,
　　Star-beam and darkness, sky and sea;
Thy face, pale in the shadowy even,
　　Thy quiet eyes that gaze on me!
Oh, realize the moment's charm,
　　Thou dearest! we are at life's best,
Folded in God's encircling arm,
　　Wave-cradled thus and wind-caressed.

## A TRYST

FROM out the desolation of the North
    An iceberg took its way,
From its detaining comrades breaking forth,
    And traveling night and day.

At whose command?   Who bade it sail the deep
    With that resistless force?
Who made the dread appointment it must keep?
    Who traced its awful course?

To the warm airs that stir in the sweet South,
    A good ship spread her sails;
Stately she passed beyond the harbor's mouth,
    Chased by the favoring gales;

And on her ample decks a happy crowd
    Bade the fair land good-by;
Clear shone the day, with not a single cloud
    In all the peaceful sky.

Brave men, sweet women, little children bright,
    For all these she made room,
And with her freight of beauty and delight
    She went to meet her doom.

Storms buffeted the iceberg, spray was swept
   Across its loftiest height;
Guided alike by storm and calm, it kept
   Its fatal path aright.

Then warmer waves gnawed at its crumbling base,
   As if in piteous plea;
The ardent sun sent slow tears down its face,
   Soft flowing to the sea.

Dawn kissed it with her tender rose tints, Eve
   Bathed it in violet,
The wistful color o'er it seemed to grieve
   With a divine regret.

Whether Day clad its clefts in rainbows dim
   And shadowy as a dream,
Or Night through lonely spaces saw it swim
   White in the moonlight's gleam,

Ever Death rode upon its solemn heights,
   Ever his watch he kept;
Cold at its heart through changing days and nights
   Its changeless purpose slept.

And where afar a smiling coast it passed,
   Straightway the air grew chill;
Dwellers thereon perceived a bitter blast,
   A vague report of ill.

Like some imperial creature, moving slow,
    Meanwhile, with matchless grace,
The stately ship, unconscious of her foe,
    Drew near the trysting place.

For still the prosperous breezes followed her,
    And half the voyage was o'er;
In many a breast glad thoughts began to stir
    Of lands that lay before.

And human hearts with longing love were dumb,
    That soon should cease to beat,
Thrilled with the hope of meetings soon to come,
    And lost in memories sweet.

Was not the weltering waste of water wide
    Enough for both to sail?
What drew the two together o'er the tide,
    Fair ship and iceberg pale?

There came a night with neither moon nor star,
    Clouds draped the sky in black;
With fluttering canvas reefed at every spar,
    And weird fire in her track,

The ship swept on; a wild wind gathering fast
    Drove her at utmost speed.
Bravely she bent before the fitful blast
    That shook her like a reed.

O helmsman, turn thy wheel!   Will no surmise
  Cleave through the midnight drear?
No warning of the horrible surprise
  Reach thine unconscious ear?

She rushed upon her ruin.   Not a flash
  Broke up the waiting dark;
Dully through wind and sea one awful crash
  Sounded, with none to mark.

Scarcely her crew had time to clutch despair,
  So swift the work was done:
Ere their pale lips could frame a speechless prayer,
  They perished, every one!


## IMPRISONED

LIGHTLY she lifts the large, pure, luminous shell,
  Poises it in her strong and shapely hand.
"Listen," she says, "it has a tale to tell,
  Spoken in language you may understand."

Smiling, she holds it at my dreaming ear:
  The old, delicious murmur of the sea
Steals like enchantment through me, and I hear
  Voices like echoes of eternity.

She stirs it softly.   Lo, another speech!
In one of its dim chambers, shut from sight,
Is sealed the water that has kissed the beach
Where the far Indian Ocean leaps in light.

Those laughing ripples, hidden evermore
In utter darkness, plaintively repeat
Their lapsing on the glowing tropic shore,
In melancholy whispers low and sweet.

O prisoned wave that may not see the sun!
O voice that never may be comforted!
You cannot break the web that Fate has spun;
Out of your world are light and gladness fled.

The red dawn nevermore shall tremble far
Across the leagues of radiant brine to you;
You shall not sing to greet the evening star,
Nor dance exulting under heaven's clear blue.

Inexorably woven is the weft
That shrouds from you all joy but memory;
Only this tender, low lament is left
Of all the sumptuous splendor of the sea.

## PRESAGE

IF, some day, I should seek those eyes
    So gentle now, — and find the strange,
    Pale shadow of a coming change,
To chill me with a sad surprise;

Shouldst thou recall what thou hast given,
    And turn me slowly cold and dumb,
    And thou thyself again become
Remote as any star in heaven;

Would the sky ever seem again
    Perfectly clear?   Would the serene,
    Sweet face of nature steal between
This grief and me, to dull its pain?

Oh not for many a weary day
    Would sorrow soften to regret,
    And many a sun would rise and set
Ere I, with cheerful heart, could say:

"All undeserved it came.   To-day,
    God takes it back again, because
    Too beautiful a thing it was
For such as I to keep for aye."

And ever, through the coming years,
  My star, remote in happy skies,
  Would seem more heavenly fair through eyes
Yet tremulous with unfallen tears.


## MIDSUMMER MIDNIGHT

THE wide, still, moonlit water miles away
  Stretches in lonely splendor.   Whispers creep
About us from the midnight wind, and play
  Among the flowers that breathe so sweet in sleep;
A soft touch sways the milk-white, stately phlox,
And on its slender stem the poppy rocks.

Fair faces turn to watch the dusky sea,
  And clear eyes brood upon the path of light
The white moon makes, the while deliciously,
  Like some vague, tender memory of delight,
Or like some half remembered, dear regret,
Rises the odor of the mignonette.

Midsummer glories, moonlight, flowers asleep,
  And delicate perfume, mystic winds that blow
Soft-breathing, full of balm, and the great deep
  In leagues of shadow swaying to and fro;
And loving human thought to mark it all,
And human hearts that to each other call;

Needs the enchantment of the summer night
 Another touch to make it perfect? Hark!
What sudden shaft of sound, like piercing light,
 Strikes on the ear athwart the moonlit dark?
Like some keen shock of joy is heard within
The wondrous music of the violin.

It is as if dumb Nature found a voice,
 And spoke with power, though in an unknown
  tongue.
What kinship has the music with the noise
 Of waves, or winds, or with the flowers, slow-swung
Like censers to and fro upon the air,
Or with the shadow, or the moonlight fair?

And yet it seems some subtile link exists,
 We know not how. And over every phase
Of thought and feeling wandering as it lists,
 Playing upon us as the west-wind plays
Over the wind-harp, the subduing strain
Sweeps with resistless power of joy and pain.

Slow ebbs the golden tide, and all is still.
 Ask the magician at whose touch awoke
That mighty, penetrating, prisoned will,
 The matchless voice that so divinely spoke,
Kindling to fresher life the listening soul,
What daring thought such fire from heaven stole?

He cannot tell us how the charm was wrought,
   Though in his hand he holds the potent key,
Nor read the spell that to the sweet night brought
   This crown of rapture and of mystery,
And lifted every heart, and drew away
All trace of worldliness that marred the day.

But every head is bowed.   We watch the sea
   With other eyes, as if some hint of bliss
Spoke to us, through the yearning melody,
   Of glad new worlds, of brighter lives than this;
While still the milk-white, stately phlox waves slow,
And drowsily the poppy rocks below.


## APRIL DAYS

Oh the sweet, sweet lapsing of the tide,
   Through the still hours of the golden afternoon!
Oh the warm, red sunshine, far and wide,
   Falling soft as in the crowning days of June!

Calls the gray sandpiper from the quiet shore,
   Weave the swallows light and music through the air,
Chants the sparrow all his pleasure o'er and o'er,
   Sings and smiles the Spring, and sparkles every-
      where.

Well I know that death and pain to all are near,
  That, save sorrow, naught is certain this world
      gives;
Yet my heart stirs with the budding of the year,
  And rejoices still with everything that lives.

Fold me then, O south-wind! God is good.
  Gladly, gratefully I take thy sweet caress.
Call, sandpiper, from thy solitude,
  Every sight and sound has power to bless.

Oh the sweet, sweet lapsing of the tide,
  Through the still hours of the golden afternoon!
Nor death, nor pain, nor sorrow shall abide,
  For God blesses all his children, late or soon.

## HEARTBREAK HILL

In Ipswich town, not far from the sea,
  Rises a hill which the people call
Heartbreak Hill, and its history
  Is an old, old legend, known to all.

The selfsame dreary, worn-out tale
  Told by all peoples in every clime,
Still to be told till the ages fail,
  And there comes a pause in the march of Time.

It was a sailor who won the heart
   Of an Indian maiden, lithe and young;
And she saw him over the sea depart,
   While sweet in her ear his promise rung;

For he cried, as he kissed her wet eyes dry,
   "I 'll come back, sweetheart; keep your faith!"
She said, "I will watch while the moons go by:"
   Her love was stronger than life or death.

So this poor dusk Ariadne kept
   Her watch from the hilltop rugged and steep;
Slowly the empty moments crept
   While she studied the changing face of the deep,

Fastening her eyes upon every speck
   That crossed the ocean within her ken;
Might not her lover be walking the deck,
   Surely and swiftly returning again?

The Isles of Shoals loomed, lonely and dim,
   In the northeast distance far and gray,
And on the horizon's uttermost rim
   The low rock heap of Boon Island lay.

And north and south and west and east
   Stretched sea and land in the blinding light,
Till evening fell, and her vigil ceased,
   And many a hearth-glow lit the night,

To mock those set and glittering eyes
 Fast growing wild as her hope went out.
Hateful seemed earth, and the hollow skies,
 Like her own heart, empty of aught but doubt.

Oh, but the weary, merciless days,
 With the sun above, with the sea afar, —
No change in her fixed and wistful gaze
 From the morning-red to the evening star!

Oh, the winds that blew, and the birds that sang,
 The calms that smiled, and the storms that rolled,
The bells from the town beneath, that rang
 Through the summer's heat and the winter's cold!

The flash of the plunging surges white,
 The soaring gull's wild, boding cry, —
She was weary of all; there was no delight
 In heaven or earth, and she longed to die.

What was it to her though the Dawn should paint
 With delicate beauty skies and seas?
But the sweet, sad sunset splendors faint
 Made her soul sick with memories:

Drowning in sorrowful purple a sail
 In the distant east, where shadows grew,
Till the twilight shrouded it, cold and pale,
 And the tide of her anguish rose anew.

Like a slender statue carved of stone
   She sat, with hardly motion or breath.
She wept no tears and she made no moan,
   But her love was stronger than life or death.

He never came back! Yet faithful still,
   She watched from the hilltop her life away.
And the townsfolk christened it Heartbreak Hill,
   And it bears the name to this very day.

## THE SONG–SPARROW

In this sweet, tranquil afternoon of spring,
   While the low sun declines in the clear west,
I sit and hear the blithe song-sparrow sing
   His strain of rapture not to be suppressed;
Pondering life's problem strange, while death draws
      near,
I listen to his dauntless song of cheer.

His shadow flits across the quiet stone:
   Like that brief transit is my space of days;
For, like a flower's faint perfume, youth is flown
   Already, and there rests on all life's ways
A dimness; closer my beloved I clasp,
For all dear things seem slipping from my grasp.

Death touches all; the light of loving eyes
   Goes out in darkness, comfort is withdrawn;
Lonely, and lonelier still the pathway lies,
   Going toward the fading sunset from the dawn:
Yet hark! while those fine notes the silence break,
As if all trouble were some grave mistake!

Thou little bird, how canst thou thus rejoice,
   As if the world had known nor sin nor curse?
God never meant to mock us with that voice!
   That is the key-note of the universe,
That song of perfect trust, of perfect cheer,
Courageous, constant, free of doubt or fear.

My little helper, ah, my comrade sweet,
   My old companion in that far-off time
When on life's threshold childhood's wingèd feet
   Danced in the sunrise!   Joy was at its prime
When all my heart responded to thy song,
Unconscious of earth's discords harsh and strong.

Now, grown aweary, sad with change and loss,
   With the enigma of myself dismayed;
Poor, save in deep desire to bear the cross
   God's hand on his defenseless creatures laid,
With patience, — here I sit this eve of spring,
And listen with bowèd head, while thou dost sing.

And slowly all my soul with comfort fills,
    And the old hope revives and courage grows;
Up the deserted shore a fresh tide thrills,
    And like a dream the dark mood melts and goes,
And with thy joy again will I rejoice:
God never meant to mock us with that voice!


## IN KITTERY CHURCHYARD

"Mary, wife of Charles Chauncy, died April 23, 1758, in the 24th
year of her age."

CRUSHING the scarlet strawberries in the grass,
I kneel to read the slanting stone.   Alas!
How sharp a sorrow speaks!   A hundred years
And more have vanished, with their smiles and tears,
Since here was laid, upon an April day,
Sweet Mary Chauncy in the grave away, —
A hundred years since here her lover stood
Beside her grave in such despairing mood,
And yet from out the vanished past I hear
His cry of anguish sounding deep and clear,
And all my heart with pity melts, as though
To-day's bright sun were looking on his woe.
"Of such a wife, O righteous Heaven! bereft,
What joy for me, what joy on earth is left?
Still from my inmost soul the groans arise,
Still flow the sorrows ceaseless from mine eyes."

Alas, poor tortured soul!   I look away
From the dark stone, — how brilliant shines the day!
A low wall, over which the roses shed
Their perfumed petals, shuts the quiet dead
Apart a little, and the tiny square
Stands in the broad and laughing field so fair,
And gay green vines climb o'er the rough stone wall,
And all about the wild birds flit and call,
And but a stone's throw southward, the blue sea
Rolls sparkling in and sings incessantly.
Lovely as any dream the peaceful place,
And scarcely changed since on her gentle face
For the last time on that sad April day
He gazed, and felt, for him, all beauty lay
Buried with her forever.   Dull to him
Looked the bright world through eyes with tears so
        dim!
"I soon shall follow the same dreary way
That leads and opens to the coasts of day."
His only hope!   But when slow time had dealt
Firmly with him and kindly, and he felt
The storm and stress of strong and piercing pain
Yielding at last, and he grew calm again,
Doubtless he found another mate before
He followed Mary to the happy shore!
But none the less his grief appeals to me
Who sit and listen to the singing sea
This matchless summer day, beside the stone

He made to echo with his bitter moan,
And in my eyes I feel the foolish tears
For buried sorrow, dead a hundred years!


## AT THE BREAKERS' EDGE

THROUGH the wide sky thy north wind's thunder
   roars
  Resistless, till no cloud is left to flee,
And down the clear, cold heaven unhindered pours
  Thine awful moonlight on the winter sea.

The vast, black, raging spaces, torn and wild,
  With an insensate fury answer back
To the gale's challenge; hurrying breakers, piled
  Each over each, roll through the glittering track.

I shudder in the terror of thy cold,
  As buffeted by the fierce blast I stand,
Watching that shining path of bronzèd gold,
  With solemn, shadowy rocks on either hand;

While at their feet, ghastly and white as death,
  The cruel, foaming billows plunge and rave.
O Father! where art Thou? My feeble breath
  Cries to Thee through the storm of wind and wave.

The cry of all thy children since the first
    That walked thy planets' myriad paths among;
The cry of all mankind whom doubt has cursed,
    In every clime, in every age and tongue.

Thou art the cold, the swift fire that consumes;
    Thy vast, unerring forces never fail;
And Thou art in the frailest flower that blooms,
    As in the breath of this tremendous gale.

Yet, though thy laws are clear as light, and prove
    Thee changeless, ever human weakness craves
Some deeper knowledge for our human love
    That looks with sad eyes o'er its wastes of graves,

And hungers for the dear hands softly drawn,
    One after one, from out our longing grasp.
Dost Thou reach out for them?   In the sweet dawn
    Of some new world thrill they within thy clasp?

Ah! what am I, thine atom, standing here
    In presence of thy pitiless elements,
Daring to question thy great silence drear,
    No voice may break to lighten our suspense!

Thou only, infinite Patience, that endures
    Forever!   Blind and dumb I cling to Thee.
Slow glides the bitter night, and silent pours
    Thine awful moonlight on the winter sea.

## "FOR THOUGHTS"

A PANSY on his breast she laid,
　　Splendid, and dark with Tyrian dyes;
　　"Take it, 't is like your tender eyes,
Deep as the midnight heaven," she said.

The rich rose mantling in her cheek,
　　Before him like the dawn she stood,
　　Pausing upon Life's height, subdued,
Yet triumphing, both proud and meek.

And white as winter stars, intense
　　With steadfast fire, his brilliant face
　　Bent toward her with an eager grace,
Pale with a rapture half suspense.

" You give me then a thought, O Sweet!"
　　He cried, and kissed the purple flower,
　　And bowed by Love's resistless power,
Trembling he sank before her feet.

She crowned his beautiful bowed head
　　With one caress of her white hand;
　　"Rise up, my flower of all the land,
For all my thoughts are yours," she said.

## WHEREFORE

BLACK sea, black sky!   A ponderous steamship driv-
   ing
   Between them, laboring westward on her way,
And in her path a trap of Death's contriving
   Waiting remorseless for its easy prey.

Hundreds of souls within her frame lie dreaming,
   Hoping and fearing, longing for the light:
With human life and thought and feeling teeming,
   She struggles onward through the starless night.

Upon her furnace fires fresh fuel flinging,
   The swarthy firemen grumble at the dust
Mixed with the coal — when suddenly upspringing,
   Swift through the smoke-stack like a signal thrust,

Flares a red flame, a dread illumination!
   A cry, — a tumult!   Slowly to her helm
The vessel yields, 'mid shouts of acclamation,
   And joy and terror all her crew o'erwhelm;

For looming from the blackness drear before them
   Discovered is the iceberg — hardly seen,
Its ghastly precipices hanging o'er them,
   Its reddened peaks, with dreadful chasms between,

Ere darkness swallows it again! and veering
   Out of its track the brave ship onward steers,
Just grazing ruin.   Trembling still, and fearing,
   Her grateful people melt in prayers and tears.

Is it a mockery, their profound thanksgiving?
   Another ship goes shuddering to her doom
Unwarned, that very night, with hopes as living
   With freight as precious, lost amid the gloom,

With not a ray to show the apparition
   Waiting to slay her, none to cry "Beware!"
Rushing straight onward headlong to perdition,
   And for her crew no time vouchsafed for prayer.

Could they have stormed Heaven's gate with anguished
      praying,
   It would not have availed a feather's weight
Against their doom.   Yet were they disobeying
   No law of God, to beckon such a fate.

And do not tell me the Almighty Master
   Would work a miracle to save the one,
And yield the other up to dire disaster,
   By merely human justice thus outdone!

Vainly we weep and wrestle with our sorrow —
   We cannot see his roads, they lie so broad:

But his eternal day knows no to-morrow,
   And life and death are all the same with God.


## GUENDOLEN

She is so fair, I thought, so dear and fair!
   Maidenly beautiful from head to feet,
   With pensive profile delicate and sweet,
And Titian's color in her sunny hair.

So fair, I thought, rejoicing even to note
   The little flexible, transparent wrist,
   The purple of the gold-clasped amethyst
That glittered at her white and slender throat;

The tiny ear, curled like a rosy shell;
   The gentle splendor of the wide brown eyes,
   Deep, lustrous, tender, clear as morning skies;
The full, sad lips, — the voice that like a bell

Rang thrilling with a music sweet and wild,
   High, airy-pure as fluting of the fays,
   Or bird-notes in the early summer days,
And joyous as the laughter of a child.

Dearest, has Heaven aught to give thee more?
   I thought, the while I watched her changing face, —

Heard her fine tones, and marked her gestures'
    grace, —
Yea, one more gift is left, all gifts before.


We go our separate ways on earth, and pain,
    God's shaping chisel, waits us as the rest,
    With nobler charm thy beauty to invest,
And make thee lovelier ere we meet again.


## THE WATCH OF BOON ISLAND

THEY crossed the lonely and lamenting sea;
    Its moaning seemed but singing. "Wilt thou
        dare,"
He asked her, "brave the loneliness with me?"
    "What loneliness," she said, "if thou art there?"


Afar and cold on the horizon's rim
    Loomed the tall lighthouse, like a ghostly sign;
They sighed not as the shore behind grew dim,
    A rose of joy they bore across the brine.


They gained the barren rock, and made their home
    Among the wild waves and the sea-birds wild;
The wintry winds blew fierce across the foam,
    But in each other's eyes they looked and smiled.

Aloft the lighthouse sent its warnings wide,
  Fed by their faithful hands, and ships in sight
With joy beheld it, and on land men cried,
  "Look, clear and steady burns Boon Island light!"

And, while they trimmed the lamp with busy hands,
  "Shine far and through the dark, sweet light!"
    they cried;
"Bring safely back the sailors from all lands
  To waiting love, — wife, mother, sister, bride!"

No tempest shook their calm, though many a storm
  Tore the vexed ocean into furious spray;
No chill could find them in their Eden warm,
  And gently Time lapsed onward day by day.

Said I no chill could find them? There is one
  Whose awful footfalls everywhere are known,
With echoing sobs, who chills the summer sun,
  And turns the happy heart of youth to stone;

Inexorable Death, a silent guest
  At every hearth, before whose footsteps flee
All joys, who rules the earth, and, without rest,
  Roams the vast shuddering spaces of the sea.

Death found them; turned his face and passed her by,
  But laid a finger on her lover's lips,

And there was silence.   Then the storm ran high,
  And tossed and troubled sore the distant ships.

Nay, who shall speak the terrors of the night,
  The speechless sorrow, the supreme despair?
Still like a ghost she trimmed the waning light,
  Dragging her slow weight up the winding stair.

With more than oil the saving lamp she fed,
  While lashed to madness the wild sea she heard.
She kept her awful vigil with the dead,
  And God's sweet pity still she ministered.

O sailors, hailing loud the cheerful beam,
  Piercing so far the tumult of the dark,
A radiant star of hope, you could not dream
  What misery there sat cherishing that spark!

Three times the night, too terrible to bear,
  Descended, shrouded in the storm.   At last
The sun rose clear and still on her despair,
  And all her striving to the winds she cast,

And bowed her head and let the light die out,
  For the wide sea lay calm as her dead love.
When evening fell, from the far land, in doubt,
  Vainly to find that faithful star men strove.

Sailors and landsmen look, and women's eyes,
　　For pity ready, search in vain the night,
And wondering neighbor unto neighbor cries,
　　"Now what, think you, can ail Boon Island light?"

Out from the coast toward her high tower they sailed;
　　They found her watching, silent, by her dead,
A shadowy woman, who nor wept, nor wailed,
　　But answered what they spake, till all was said.

They bore the dead and living both away.
　　With anguish time seemed powerless to destroy
She turned, and backward gazed across the bay, —
　　Lost in the sad sea lay her rose of joy.

## BEETHOVEN

### I

O SOVEREIGN Master! stern and splendid power,
　　That calmly dost both Time and Death defy;
Lofty and lone as mountain peaks that tower,
　　Leading our thoughts up to the eternal sky:
Keeper of some divine, mysterious key,
　　Raising us far above all human care,
Unlocking awful gates of harmony
　　To let heaven's light in on the world's despair;
Smiter of solemn chords that still command

Echoes in souls that suffer and aspire,
In the great moment while we hold thy hand,
  Baptized with pain and rapture, tears and fire,
God lifts our saddened foreheads from the dust,
The everlasting God, in whom we trust!

## II

O stateliest! who shall speak thy praise, who find
  A fitting word to utter before thee?
Thou lonely splendor, thou consummate mind,
  Who marshalest thy hosts in majesty;
Thy shadowy armies of resistless thought,
  Thy subtile forces drawn from Nature's heart,
Thy solemn breathing, mighty music, wrought
  Of life and death — a miracle thou art!
The restless tides of human life that swing
  In stormy currents, thou dost touch and sway;
Deep tones within us answer, shuddering,
  At thy resounding voice — we cast away
All our unworthiness, made strong by thee,
Thou great uplifter of humanity!

## III

And was it thus the master looked, think you?
  Is this the painter's fancy?   Who can tell!
These strong and noble outlines should be true:
  On the broad brow such majesty should dwell.

Yea, and these deep, indomitable eyes
    Are surely his.    Lo, the imperial will
In every feature!    Mighty purpose lies
    About the shut mouth, resolute and still.
Observe the head's pathetic attitude,
    Bent forward, listening, — he that might not hear!
Ah, could the world's adoring gratitude,
    So late to come, have made his life less drear!
Hearest thou, now, great soul beyond our ken,
Men's reverent voices answering thee, "Amen"?


## MOZART

Most beautiful among the helpers thou!
    All heaven's fresh air and sunshine at thy voice
Flood with refreshment many a weary brow,
    And sad souls thrill with courage and rejoice
To hear God's gospel of pure gladness sound
    So sure and clear in this bewildered world,
Till the sick vapors that our sense confound
    By cheerful winds are into nothing whirled.
O matchless melody!    O perfect art!
    O lovely, lofty voice, unfaltering!
O strong and radiant and divine Mozart,
    Among earth's benefactors crowned a king!
Loved shalt thou be while time may yet endure,
Spirit of health, sweet, sound, and wise, and pure.

## SCHUBERT

At the open window I lean;
 Flowers in the garden without
 Faint in the heat and the drought;
What does the music mean?

For here, from the cold keys within,
 Is a tempest of melody drawn;
 Doubts, passionate questions, the dawn
Of high hope, and a triumph to win;

While out in the garden, blood-red
 The poppy droops, faint in the heat
 Of the noon, and the sea-wind so sweet
Caresses its delicate head.

And still the strong music goes on
 With its storming of beautiful heights,
 With its sorrow that heaven requites,
And the victory fought for is won!

High with thy gift didst thou reach,
 Schubert, whose genius superb
 Nothing could check or could curb:
Thou liftest the heart with thy speech!

## CHOPIN

CALM is the close of the day,
  All things are quiet and blest;
  Low in the darkening west
The young moon sinks slowly away.

Without, in the twilight, I dream:
  Within it is cheerful and bright
  With faces that bloom in the light,
And the cold keys that silently gleam.

Then a magical touch draws near,
  And a voice like a call of delight
  Cleaves the calm of the beautiful night,
And I turn from my musing to hear.

Lo! the movement too wondrous to name!
  Agitation and rapture, the press
  As of myriad waves that caress,
And break into vanishing flame.

Ah! but the exquisite strain,
  Sinking to pathos so sweet!
  Is life then a lie and a cheat?
Hark to the hopeless refrain!

Comes a shock like the voice of a soul
   Lost to good, to all beauty and joy,
   Led alone by the powers that destroy,
And fighting with fiends for control.

Drops a chord like the grave's first clod.
   Then again toss the waves of caprice,
   Wild, delicate, sweet, with no peace,
No health, and no yielding to God.

O Siren, that charmest the air
   With this potent and passionate spell,
   Sad as songs of the angels that fell,
Thou leadest alone to despair!

What troubles the night?  It grows chill —
   Let the weird, wild music be;
   Fronts us the infinite sea
And Nature is holy and still.

## THE PIMPERNEL

SHE walks beside the silent shore,
   The tide is high, the breeze is still;
No ripple breaks the ocean floor,
   The sunshine sleeps upon the hill.

The turf is warm beneath her feet,
　Bordering the beach of stone and shell,
And thick about her path the sweet
　Red blossoms of the pimpernel.

"Oh, sleep not yet, my flower!" she cries,
　"Nor prophesy of storm to come;
Tell me that under steadfast skies
　Fair winds shall bring my lover home."

She stoops to gather flower and shell,
　She sits, and, smiling, studies each;
She hears the full tide rise and swell,
　And whisper softly on the beach.

Waking, she dreams a golden dream,
　Remembering with what still delight,
To watch the sunset's fading gleam,
　Here by the waves they stood last night.

She leans on that encircling arm,
　Divinely strong with power to draw
Her nature, as the moon doth charm
　The swaying sea with heavenly law.

All lost in bliss the moments glide;
　She feels his whisper, his caress;
The murmur of the mustering tide
　Brings her no presage of distress.

What breaks her dream? She lifts her eyes
    Reluctant to destroy the spell;
The color from her bright cheek dies, —
    Close folded is the pimpernel.

With rapid glance she scans the sky;
    Rises a sudden wind, and grows,
And charged with storm the cloud-heaps lie.
    Well may the scarlet blossoms close!

A touch, and bliss is turned to bale!
    Life only keeps the sense of pain;
The world holds naught save one white sail
    Flying before the wind and rain.

Broken upon the wheel of fear
    She wears the storm-vexed hour away;
And now in gold and fire draws near
    The sunset of her troubled day.

But to her sky is yet denied
    The sun that lights the world for her;
She sweeps the rose-flushed ocean wide
    With eager eyes the quick tears blur;

And lonely, lonely all the space
    Stretches, with never sign of sail,
And sadder grows her wistful face,
    And all the sunset splendors fail.

And cold and pale, in still despair,
 With heavier grief than tongue can tell,
She sinks, — upon her lips a prayer,
 Her cheek against the pimpernel.

Bright blossoms wet with showery tears
 On her shut eyes their droplets shed.
Only the wakened waves she hears,
 That, singing, drown his rapid tread.

"Sweet, I am here!"  Joy's gates swing wide,
 And heaven is theirs, and all is well,
And left beside the ebbing tide,
 Forgotten, is the pimpernel.

## BY THE DEAD

O Poverty! till now I never knew
 The meaning of the word!  What lack is here!
O pale mask of a soul great, good, and true!
 O mocking semblance stretched upon a bier!

Each atom of this devastated face
 Was so instinct with power, with warmth and
  light;
What desert is so desolate!  No grace
 Is left, no gleam, no change, no day, no night.

Where is the key that locked these gates of speech,
    Once beautiful, where thought stood sentinel,
Where sweetness sat, where wisdom passed, to teach
    Our weakness strength, our homage to compel?

Despoiled at last, and waste and barren lies
    This once so rich domain.   Where lives and moves,
In what new world, the splendor of these eyes
    That dauntless lightened like imperial Jove's?

Annihilated, do you answer me?
    Blown out and vanished like a candle flame?
Is nothing left but this pale effigy,
    This silence drear, this dread without a name?

Has it been all in vain, our love and pride,
    This yearning love that still pursues our friend
Into the awful dark, unsatisfied,
    Bereft, and wrung with pain?   Is this the end?

Would God so mock us?   To our human sense
    No answer reaches through the doubtful air;
Yet with a living hope, profound, intense,
    Our tortured souls rebel against despair;

As bowing to the bitter fate we go
    Drooping and dumb as if beneath a curse;
But does not pitying Heaven answer "No!"
    With all the voices of the universe?

## FOOTPRINTS IN THE SAND

LAZILY, through the warm gray afternoon,
    We sailed toward the land;
Over the long sweep of the billows, soon,
    We saw on either hand
Peninsula and cape and silver beach
    Unfold before our eyes,
Lighthouse and roof and spire and wooded reach
    Grew clear beyond surmise.
Behind us lay the islands that we loved,
    Touched by a wandering gleam,
Melting in distance, where the white sails moved
    Softly as in a dream.
Drifting past buoy and scarlet beacon slow,
    We gained the coast at last,
And up the harbor, where no wind did blow,
    We drew, and anchor cast.
The lovely land!  Green, the broad fields came down
    Almost into the sea;
Nestled the quiet homesteads warm and brown,
    Embraced by many a tree;
The gray above was streaked with smiling blue,
    The snowy gulls sailed o'er;
The shining goldenrod waved, where it grew,
    A welcome to the shore.
Peaceful the whole, and sweet.  Beyond the sand
    The dwelling-place I sought

Lay in the sunshine.   All the scene I scanned,
   Full of one wistful thought:
Saw any eyes our vessel near the shore
   From vine-draped windows quaint?
Waited my bright, shy darling at the door,
   Fairer than words could paint?
I did not see her gleaming golden head,
   Nor hear her clear voice call;
As up the beach I went with rapid tread,
   Lonely and still was all.
But on the smooth sand printed, far and near,
   I saw her footsteps small;
Here had she loitered, here she hastened, here
   She climbed the low stone wall.
Such pathos in those little footprints spoke,
   I paused and lingered long;
Listening as far away the billows broke
   With the old solemn song.
"The infinite hoary spray of the salt sea,"
   In yet another tide,
Should wash away these traces utterly;
   And in my heart I cried, —
"O thou Creator, when thy waves of Time,
   The infinite hoary spray
That sweeps life from the earth at dawn and prime,
   Have swept her soul away,
How shall I know it is not even as these
   Light footprints in the sand,

That vanish into naught? For no man sees
    Clearly what Thou hast planned."
And sadly musing, up the slope I pressed,
    And sought her where she played,
By breeze and sunshine flattered and caressed,
    A merry little maid.
And while I clasped her close and held her fast,
    And looked into her face,
Half shy, half smiling, wholly glad at last
    To rest in my embrace,
From the clear heaven of her innocent eyes
    Leaped Love to answer me;
Divinely thro' 'h the mortal shape that dies
    Shone immortality!
What the winds hinted, what the awful sky
    Held in its keeping, — all
The vast sea's prophesying suddenly
    Grew clear as clarion call.
The secret nature strives to speak, yet hides,
    Flashed from those human eyes
To slay my doubt: I felt that all the tides
    Of death and change might rise
And devastate the world, yet I could see
    This steady shining spark
Should live eternally, could never be
    Lost in the unfathomed dark!
And when beneath a threatening sunset sky
    We trimmed our sails and turned

Seaward again, with many a sweet good-by,
  A quiet gladness burned
Within me, as I watched her tiny form
  Go dancing up and down,
Light as a sandpiper before the storm,
  Upon the beach-edge brown,
Waving her little kerchief to and fro
  Till we were out of sight,
Sped by a wild wind that began to blow
  Out of the troubled night;
And while we tossed upon an angry sea,
  And round the lightning ran,
And muttering thunder rolled incessantly
  As the black storm began,
I knew the fair and peaceful landscape lay
  Safe hidden in the gloom,
Waiting the glad returning of the day
  To smile again and bloom;
And sure as that to-morrow's sun would rise,
  And day again would be,
Shone the sweet promise of those childish eyes
  Wherein God answered me.


## A BROKEN LILY

O LILY, dropped upon the gray sea-sand,
What time my fair love through the morning land
Led the rejoicing children, singing all

In happy chorus, to their festival,
Under green trees the flowery fields among;
  Now, when the noon sun blazes o'er the sea,
And echo tells not of the song they sung,
  And all thy silver splendor silently
Thou yieldest to the salt and bitter tide,
  I find thee, and, remembering on whose breast
Thy day began in thy fresh beauty's pride,
  Though of thy bloom and fragrance dispossessed,
Thou art to me than all June's flowers more sweet,
Fairer than Aphrodite's foam-kissed feet!


## MAY MORNING

WARM, wild, rainy wind, blowing fitfully,
Stirring dreamy breakers on the slumberous May sea,
What shall fail to answer thee? What thing shall
      withstand
The spell of thine enchantment, flowing over sea and
      land?


All along the swamp-edge in the rain I go;
All about my head thou the loosened locks dost blow;
Like the German goose-girl in the fairy tale,
I watch across the shining pool my flock of ducks that
      sail.

Redly gleam the rose-haws, dripping with the wet,
Fruit of sober autumn, glowing crimson yet;
Slender swords of iris leaves cut the water clear,
And light green creeps the tender grass, thick spread-
    ing far and near.

Every last year's stalk is set with brown or golden
    studs;
All the boughs of bayberry are thick with scented
    buds;
Islanded in turfy velvet, where the ferns uncurl,
Lo! the large white duck's egg glimmers like a pearl!

Softly sing the billows, rushing, whispering low;
Freshly, oh! deliciously, the warm, wild wind doth
    blow!
Plaintive bleat of new-washed lambs comes faint from
    far away;
And clearly cry the little birds, alert and blithe and
    gay.

O happy, happy morning! O dear, familiar place!
O warm, sweet tears of Heaven, fast falling on my
    face!
O well-remembered, rainy wind, blow all my care
    away,
That I may be a child again this blissful morn of May.

## ALL 'S WELL

WHAT dost thou here, young wife, by the water-side,
  Gathering crimson dulse?
Know'st thou not that the cloud in the west glooms
      wide,
  And the wind has a hurrying pulse?

Peaceful the eastern waters before thee spread,
  And the cliffs rise high behind,
While thou gatherest sea-weeds, green and brown and
      red,
  To the coming trouble blind.

She lifts her eyes to the top of the granite crags,
  And the color ebbs from her cheek,
Swift vapors skurry the black squall's tattered flags,
  And she hears the gray gull shriek.

And like a blow is the thought of the little boat
  By this on its homeward way,
A tiny skiff, like a cockle-shell afloat
  In the tempest-threatened bay;

With husband and brother who sailed away to the
      town
  When fair shone the morning sun,

To tarry but till the tide in the stream turned down,
  Then seaward again to run.

Homeward she flies; the land-breeze strikes her cold;
  A terror is in the sky;
Her little babe with his tumbled hair of gold
  In her mother's arms doth lie.

She catches him up with a breathless, questioning cry:
  "O mother, speak!  Are they near?"
"Dear, almost home.  At the western window high
  Thy father watches in fear."

She climbs the stair: "O father, must they be lost?"
  He answers never a word;
Through the glass he watches the line the squall has
      crossed
  As if no sound he heard.

And the Day of Doom seems come in the angry sky,
  And a low roar fills the air;
In an awful stillness the dead-black waters lie,
  And the rocks gleam ghastly and bare.

Is it a snow-white gull's wing fluttering there,
  In the midst of that hush of dread?
Ah, no, 't is the narrow strip of canvas they dare
  In the face of the storm to spread.

A moment more and all the furies are loose,
   The coast line is blotted out,
The skiff is gone, the rain-cloud pours its sluice,
   And she hears her father shout,

"Down with your sail! as if through the tumult
     wild,"
   And the distance, his voice might reach;
And, stunned, she clasps still closer her rosy child,
   Bereft of the power of speech.

But her heart cries low, as writhing it lies on the
     rack,
   "Sweet, art thou fatherless?"
And swift to her mother she carries the little one
     back,
   Where she waits in her sore distress.

Then into the heart of the storm she rushes forth;
   Like leaden bullets the rain
Beats hard in her face, and the hurricane from the
     north
   Would drive her back again.

It splits the shingles off the roof like a wedge,
   It lashes her clothes and her hair,
But slowly she fights her way to the western ledge,
   With the strength of her despair.

Through the flying spray, through the rain-cloud's
    shattered stream,
  What shapes in the distance grope,
Like figures that haunt the shore of a dreadful dream?
  She is wild with a desperate hope.

Have pity, merciful Heaven! Can it be?
  Is it no vision that mocks?
From billow to billow the headlong plunging sea
  Has tossed them high on the rocks;

And the hollow skiff like a child's toy lies on the
    ledge
  This side of the roaring foam,
And up from the valley of death, from the grave's
    drear edge,
  Like ghosts of men they come!

Oh sweetly, sweetly shines the sinking sun,
  And the storm is swept away;
Piled high in the east are the cloud-heaps purple and
    dun,
  And peacefully dies the day.

But a sweeter peace falls soft on the grateful souls
  In the lonely isle that dwell,
And the whisper and rush of every wave that rolls
  Seem murmuring, "All is well."

## THE SECRET

"Oh what saw you, gathering flowers so early this
    May morn?"
"I saw a shining blackbird loud whistling on a thorn;
I saw the mottled plover from the swamp-edge fly
    away;
I heard the blithe song-sparrows who welcomed the
    bright day;
I heard the curlew calling, oh, sweet, so sweet and far!
I saw the white gull twinkling in the blue sky like a
    star."


"And is the blackbird whistling yet, and does the
    curlew call,
And should I find your rapture if I saw and heard it
    all?
Life seems to me so hard to bear, perplexed with
    change and loss,
Heavy with pain, and weary still with care's perpetual
    cross,
Why should the white gull's twinkling wings, half
    lost amid the blue,
Bring any joy? Yet care and pain weigh just as
    much on you,
And you come back and look at me with such joy-
    beaming eyes

An angel might have been your guide through fields
 of Paradise!
What is the secret Nature keeps to whisper in your ear
That sends the swift blood pulsing warm with such
 immortal cheer,
And makes your eyes shine like the morn, and rings
 sweet in your voice,
Like some clear, distant trumpet sound that bids the
 world rejoice?"
"Her secret? Nay, she speaks to me no word you
 might not hear.
Her voice is ever ready and her meaning ever clear:
But I love her with such passion that her lightest ges-
 ture seems
Divinely beautiful — she fills my life with golden
 dreams.
I tremble in her presence, to her every touch and tone;
I answer to her whisper — love has to worship grown.
She turns her solemn face to me, and lays within my
 hand
The key that puts her endless wealth for aye at my
 command;
And so, because I worship her, her benedictions rest
Upon me, and she folds me safe and warm upon her
 breast,
And in her sweet and awful eyes I gaze till I forget
The troubles that perplex our days, the tumult and
 the fret.

Oh, would you learn the word of power that lifts, all
    care above,
The sad soul up to Nature's heart?  I answer, It is
    Love!"

## SEASIDE GOLDENROD

GRACEFUL, tossing plume of glowing gold,
    Waving lonely on the rocky ledge;
Leaning seaward, lovely to behold,
    Clinging to the high cliff's ragged edge;

Burning in the pure September sky,
    Spike of gold against the stainless blue,
Do you watch the vessels drifting by?
    Does the quiet day seem long to you?

Up to you I climb, O perfect shape!
    Poised so lightly 'twixt the sky and sea;
Looking out o'er headland, crag, and cape,
    O'er the ocean's vague immensity.

Up to you my human thought I bring,
    Sit me down your peaceful watch to share.
Do you hear the waves below us sing?
    Feel you the soft fanning of the air?

How much of life's rapture is your right?
　In earth's joy what may your portion be?
Rocked by breezes, touched by tender light,
　Fed by dews and sung to by the sea!

Something of delight and of content
　Must be yours, however vaguely known;
And your grace is mutely eloquent,
　And your beauty makes the rock a throne.

Matters not to you, O golden flower!
　That such eyes of worship watch you sway;
But you make more sweet the dreamful hour
　And you crown for me the tranquil day.


## MARCH

　THE keen north wind pipes loud;
　Swift scuds the flying cloud;
　Light lies the new fallen snow;
　The ice-clad eaves drip slow,
　For glad Spring has begun,
　And to the ardent sun
　The earth, long time so bleak,
　Turns a frost-bitten cheek.
　Through the clear sky of March,
　Blue to the topmost arch,

Swept by the New Year's gales,
The crow, harsh-clamoring, sails.
By the swift river's flood
The willow's golden blood
Mounts to the highest spray,
More vivid day by day;
And fast the maples now
Crimson through every bough,
And from the alder's crown
Swing the long catkins brown.
Gone is the winter's pain;
Though sorrow still remain,
Though eyes with tears be wet,
The voice of our regret
We hush, to hear the sweet
Far fall of summer's feet.
The Heavenly Father wise
Looks in the saddened eyes
Of our unworthiness,
Yet doth He cheer and bless.
Doubt and Despair are dead;
Hope dares to raise her head,
And whispers of delight
Fill the earth day and night.
The snowdrops by the door
Lift upward, sweet and pure,
Their delicate bells; and soon,
In the calm blaze of noon,

By lowly window-sills
Will laugh the daffodils!


## SONG

THE clover blossoms kiss her feet,
  She is so sweet,
While I, who may not kiss her hand,
Bless all the wild flowers in the land.

Soft sunshine falls across her breast,
  She is so blest.
I 'm jealous of its arms of gold,
Oh that these arms her form might fold!

Gently the breezes kiss her hair,
  She is so fair.
Let flowers and sun and breeze go by,
O dearest!   Love me or I die.

OSCAR LAIGHTON


## THE WHITE ROVER

THEY called the little schooner the White Rover,
  When they lightly launched her on the brimming
      tide;
Stanch and trim she was to sail the broad seas over,
  And with cheers they spread her snowy canvas wide;

And a thing of beauty, forth she fared to wrestle
　　With the wild, uncertain ocean, far and near,
And no evil thing befell the graceful vessel,
　　And she sailed in storm and sunshine many a year.

But at last a rumor grew that she was haunted;
　　That up her slender masts her sails had flown
Unhelped by human hands, as if enchanted,
　　As she rocked upon her moorings all alone.

Howe'er that be, one day in winter weather,
　　When the bitter north was raging at its worst,
And wind and cold vexed the roused sea together,
　　Till Dante's frozen hell seemed less accurst,

Two fishermen, to draw their trawls essaying,
　　Seized by the hurricane that ploughed the bay,
Were swept across the waste; and hardly weighing
　　Death's chance, the Rover reefed and bore away

To save them, — reached them, shuddering where they
　　　　waited
　　Their quick destruction, tossing white and dumb,
And caught them from perdition; then, belated,
　　Strove to return the rough way she had come.

But there was no returning!　Fierce as lightning
　　The eager cold grew keener, more intense.

Across her homeward track the billows, whitening,
  In crested mountains rolling, drove her thence;

Till her brave crew, benumbed, gave up the battle,
  Clad in a mail of ice that weighed like lead;
They heard the crusted blocks and rigging rattle,
  They saw the sails like sheets of iron spread.

And powerless before the gale they drifted,
  Till swiftly dropped the black and hopeless night.
The wild tornado never lulled nor shifted,
  But drove them toward the coast upon their right,

And flung the frozen schooner, all sail standing,
  Stiff as an iceberg on the icy shore;
And half alive, her torpid people, landing,
  Crept to the lighthouse, and were safe once more.

Then what befell the vessel, standing solemn
  Through that tremendous night of cold and storm,
Upon the frost-locked land, a frigid column,
  Beneath the stars, a silent, glittering form?

None ever saw her more!  The tide upbore her,
  Released her fastened keel, and ere the day,
Without a guide, and all the world before her,
  The sad, forsaken Rover sailed away.

But sometimes, when in summer twilight blending
    Sunset and moonrise mingle their rich light,
Or when on noonday mists the sun is spending
    His glory, till they glimmer thin and white,

Upon the dim horizon melting, gleaming,
    Slender, ethereal, like a lovely ghost
Soft looming, in the hazy distance dreaming,
    Or gliding like a film along the coast,

I seem to see her yet: and skippers hoary,
    Sailors and fishermen, will still relate
Among their sea-worn mates the simple story
    Of how the wandering Rover met her fate;

And shake their heads: "Perhaps the tempest wrecked
        her,
    But snug and trim and tidy, fore and aft,
I've seen the vessel since, or else her spectre,
    Sailing as never yet sailed earthly craft,

Straight in the wind's teeth; and with steady mo-
        tion
    Cleaving a calm as if it blew a gale!"
And they are sure her wraith still haunts the ocean,
    Mocking the sight with semblance of a sail.

## CONTRAST

THE day is bitter.   Through the hollow sky
  Rolls the clear sun, inexorably bright,
Glares on the shrinking earth, a lidless eye,
  Shedding no warmth, but floods of blinding light.

The hurricane roars loud.   The facile sea
  With passionate resentment writhes and raves
Beneath its maddening whip, and furiously
  Responds with all the thunder of its waves.

The iron rock, ice-locked, snow-sheathed, lies still,
  The centre of this devastated world,
Beaten and lashed by wind and sea at will,
  Buried in spray by the fierce breakers hurled.

Cold, raging desolation!   Out of it,
  Swift-footed, eager, noiseless as the light,
Glides my adventurous thought, and lo, I sit
  With Memnon and the desert in my sight.

Silence and breathless heat!   A torrid land,
  Unbroken to the vast horizon's verge,
Save once, where from the waste of level sand
  All motionless the clustered palms emerge.

Hot the wide earth and hot the blazing sky,
   And still as death, unchanged since time began.
Far in the shimmering distance silently
   Creeps like a snake the lessening caravan.

And on the great lips of the statue old
   Broods silence, and no zephyr stirs the palm.
Nature forgets her tempests and her cold,
   And breathes in peace. "There is no joy but
     calm."


## A FADED GLOVE

My little granddaughter, who fain would know
   Why, folded close in scented satin fine,
I keep a relic faded long ago,
   This pearl-gray, dainty, withered glove of mine,

Listen: I'll tell you. It is fifty years
   Since the fair day I laid my treasure here.
But yesterday to me the time appears;
   Ages ago to you, I know, my dear.

Upon this palm, now withered as my cheek,
   Love laid his first kiss, doubting and afraid:
Oh, swift and strong across me while I speak
   Comes memory of Love's might, my little maid!

I yet was so unconscious! 'T was a night —
  Some festal night; my sisters were above,
Not ready quite; but I, cloaked all in white,
  Waited below, and, fastening my glove,

Looked up with smiling speech to him who stood
  Observing me, so still and so intent,
I wondered somewhat at his quiet mood,
  Till it flashed on me what the silence meant.

What sudden fire of dawn my sky o'erspread!
  What low melodious thunder broke my calm!
Could I be dreaming that this glorious head
  Was bending low above my girlish palm?

His majesty of mien proclaimed him king;
  His lowly gesture said, "I am your slave;"
Beneath my feet the firm earth seemed to swing,
  Unstable as storm-driven wind and wave.

Ah, beautiful and terrible and sweet
  The matchless moment! Was it life or death,
Or day or night? For my heart ceased to beat,
  And heaven and earth changed in a single breath.

And, like a harp some hand of power doth smite
  To sudden harmony, my soul awoke,
And, answering, rose to match his spirit's height,
  While not a word the mystic silence broke.

'T was but an instant.　Down the echoing stair
　　Swept voices, laughter, wafts of melody, —
My sisters three, in draperies light as air;
　　But like a dream the whole world seemed to me,

As, steadying my whirling thoughts, I strove
　　To grasp a truth so wondrous, so divine.
I shut this hand, this little tinted glove,
　　To keep its secret mine, and only mine.

And like an empty show the brilliant hours
　　Passed by, with beauty, music, pleasure thronged,
Phantasmagoria of light and flowers;
　　But only one delight to me belonged,

One thought, one wish, one hope, one joy, one fear,
　　One dizzy rapture, one star in the sky, —
The solemn sky that bent to bring God near:
　　I would have been content that night to die.

Only a touch upon this little glove,
　　And, lo, the lofty marvel which it wrought!
You wonder; for as yet you know not love,
　　Oh, sweet my child, my lily yet unsought!

The glove is faded, but immortal joy
　　Lives in the kiss; its memory cannot fade;
And when Death's clasp this pale hand shall destroy,
　　The sacred glove shall in my grave be laid.

## PORTENT

WHEN the darkness drew away at the dawning of the
day,
I heard the medricks screaming loud and shrill across
the bay;
And I wondered to behold all the sky in ruddy gold,
Flashing into fire and flame where the clouds like bil-
lows rolled.


Red the sea ran east and west, burning broke each
tumbling crest,
Where the waves, like shattered rubies, leaped and
fell and could not rest;
Every rock was carmine-flushed, every sail like roses
blushed,
Flying swift before the wind from the south that
roared and rushed.


"Is it judgment day?" I said, gazing out o'er billows
red,
Gazing up at crimson vapors, crowding, drifting over-
head,
Listening to the great uproar of the waters on the
shore,
To the wild sad-crying sea-birds, buffeted and beaten
sore.

"Is the end of time at hand? is this pageant, strange
     and grand,
A portent of destruction blazing fierce o'er sea and
     land?"
Then the scarlet ebbed, and slow, sky above and earth
     below,
Drowned in melancholy purple, seemed with grief to
     overflow.


And while thus I gazed, the day, growing stronger,
     turned to gray;
All the transitory splendor and the beauty passed
     away;
And I recognized the sign of the color poured like
     wine
In this morn of late October as from clusters of the
     vine.


'Twas the ripeness of the year; soon, I knew, must
     disappear
All the warmth and light and happiness that made the
     time so dear;
And again our souls must wait while the bare earth,
     desolate,
Bore in patience and in silence all the winter's wrath
     and hate.

## SONG

Sing, little bird, oh sing!
  How sweet thy voice and clear!
How fine the airy measures ring,
  The sad old world to cheer!

Bloom, little flower, oh bloom!
  Thou makest glad the day;
A scented torch, thou dost illume
  The darkness of the way.

Dance, little child, oh dance!
  While sweet the small birds sing,
And flowers bloom fair, and every glance
  Of sunshine tells of spring.

Oh! bloom, and sing, and smile,
  Child, bird, and flower, and make
The sad old world forget awhile
  Its sorrow for your sake!

## RENUNCIATION

LIKE scattered flowers blown all about the bay,
 The rosy sails, lit with the sunrise, shine;
The white stars in the brightness fade away;
 In perfect silence dawns the day divine.

"Oh bring me neither gifts of good or ill,
 Delicious day! Let only peace be mine!"
And the fair hours, advancing calm and still,
 Passed by her mute, nor brought her word or sign.

But when the glory of the sunset flame
 Held all the world in triumph brief and sweet,
The last bright hour, with faltering footsteps, came
 And laid a gift august before her feet.

Yet she entreated, "Peace! Take back your gift,
 O golden hour! I am content to be
Lonely as yonder fading sails that drift
 'Neath saddened skies upon the silent sea."

Fate answered her, "The gods may not recall
 Their gifts, once given. Be wise, therefore. Ac-
  cept
Their bounty gratefully; for not to all
 Such largess falls." She bowed her head and wept.

She turned her from the sunset's red and gold,
　She faced the dim East's waning violet,
She saw the twilight stealing pale and cold,
　And all her soul was wrung with her regret.

Pure, powerful, triumphant music shook
　The listening air and floated up the sky;
The dust and ashes of her life she took
　And passed the gift of splendid beauty by.

"But oh, must storm and strife be mine," she cried,
　"Forever?　Shall I never find repose?
Mocked by mirage of hope and still defied
　And buffeted by every wind that blows!"

From farthest distance high a clear voice rang,
　"Ashes and dust shall blossom like the rose!
Climb thou above the tempests," sweet it sang;
　"Patience!　'On every height there lies repose.'"


## SONG

Oн the fragrance of the air
　With the breathing of the flowers!
Oh the isles of cloudlets fair,
　Shining after balmy showers!

Oh the freshly rippling notes!
　　Oh the warbling, loud and long,
From a thousand golden throats!
　　Oh the south wind's tender song!

Oh the mellow dip of oars
　　Through the dreamy afternoon!
Oh the waves that clasp the shores,
　　Chanting one delicious tune!

Wears the warm, enchanted day
　　To the last of its rich hours,
While my heart, in the sweet May,
　　Buds and blossoms with the flowers.

## TWO SONNETS

Not so!   You stand as long ago a king
　　Stood on the seashore, bidding back the tide
That onward rolled resistless still, to fling
　　Its awful volume landward, wild and wide.
And just as impotent is your command
　　To stem the tide that rises in my soul.
It ebbs not at the lifting of your hand,
　　It owns no curb, it yields to no control;
Mighty it is, and of the elements, —
　　Brother of winds and lightning, cold and fire,

Subtle as light, as steadfast and intense;
  Sweet as the music of Apollo's lyre.
You think to rule the ocean's ebb and flow
With that soft woman's hand? Nay, love, not so.


And like the lighthouse on the rock you stand,
  And pierce the distance with your searching eyes;
Nor do you heed the waves that storm the land
  And endlessly about you fall and rise,
But seek the ships that wander night and day
  Within the dim horizon's shadowy ring;
And some with flashing glance you warn away,
  And some you beckon with sweet welcoming.
So steadfast still you keep your lofty place,
  Safe from the tumult of the restless tide,
Firm as the rock in your resisting grace,
  And strong through humble duty, not through
      pride.
While I — I cast my life before your feet,
And only live that I may love you, sweet!


## DAYBREAK

In the morning twilight, while the household yet
Slumbering securely day and night forget,
Lightly o'er the threshold I pass, and breathless stand
In the dream of beauty that rests on sea and land.

Fresh and calm and dewy, bathed in delicate air,
The happy earth awakens and grows of day aware.
Sweetly breaks the silence some bird's delicious trill,
And from the southern distance a breeze begins to
      thrill.

All the stars have faded, and the low large moon
O'er the western water will have vanished soon.
Crystal-clear and cloudless the awful arch is bright,
As up the conscious heaven streams the growing light.

On the far horizon softly sleeps the haze;
O'er the ocean spaces steal the rosy rays;
Winds and waves are quiet, only far away
'Gainst the rock a breaker tosses sudden spray.

Out behind the headland glides the coaster slow,
All her canvas blushing in the ruddy glow;
Where the steadfast lighthouse watches day and night,
Beautiful and stately she passes out of sight.

Day that risest splendid, with promise so divine,
Mine is thy perfect gladness, thy loveliness is mine.
Thou touchest with thy blessing God's creatures great
      and small;
None shalt thou find more grateful than I among them
      all.

I turn my face in worship to the glory of the East.
I thank the lavish giver of my life's perpetual feast,
And fain would I be worthy to partake of Nature's
    bliss,
And share with her a moment so exquisite as this!


## SONG

    O LOVE, Love, Love!
  Whether it rain or shine,
Whether the clouds frown or the sky is clear,
Whether the thunder fill the air with fear,
Whether the winter rage or peace is here,
    If only thou art near,
    Then are all days divine.

    O Love, Love, Love!
  Where thou art not, the place
Is sad to me as death.   It would be cold
In heaven without thee, if I might not hold
Thy hand in mine, if I might not behold
    The beauty manifold,
    The wonder of thy face.

## THE NESTLING SWALLOWS

THE summer day was spoiled with fitful storm;
    At night the wind died, and the soft rain dropped
With lulling murmur, and the air was warm,
    And all the tumult and the trouble stopped.

We sat within the bright and quiet room,
    Glowing with light and flowers and friendliness;
And faces in the radiance seemed to bloom,
    Touched into beauty as by a caress.

And one struck music from the ivory keys, —
    Beethoven's music; and the awful chords
Upbore us like the waves of mighty seas
    That sing aloud, "All glory is the Lord's!"

And the great sound awoke beneath the eaves
    The nestling swallows; and their twittering cry,
With the light touch of raindrops on the leaves,
    Broke into the grand surging melody.

Across its deep, tremendous questioning,
    Its solemn acquiescence, low and clear,
The rippling notes ran sweet, with airy ring
    Surprised, inquiring, but devoid of fear;

Lapsing to silence at the music's close,
  A dreamy clamor, a contented stir.
"It made no discord," smiling, as he rose,
  Said the great master's great interpreter.

No discord, truly!  Ever Nature weaves
  Her sunshine with her shadow, joy with pain:
The asking thunder through high heaven that cleaves
  Is lost in the low ripple of the rain.

About the edges of the dread abyss
  The innocent blossoms laugh toward the sun;
Questions of life and death, of bale or bliss,
  A thousand tender touches overrun.

Why should I chronicle so slight a thing?
  But such things light up life like wayside flowers,
And memory, like a bird with folded wing,
  Broods with still joy o'er such delicious hours.

Dear unforgotten time!  Fair summer night!
  Thy nestling swallows and thy dropping rain,
The golden music and the faces bright,
  Will steal with constant sweetness back again.

A joy to keep when winter darkness comes;
  A living sense of beauty to recall;
A warm, bright thought, when bitter cold benumbs,
  To make me glad and grateful.   That is all.

## VESPER SONG

Lies the sunset splendor far and wide,
          On the golden tide!
Drifting slow toward yonder evening red,
With the faint stars sparkling overhead,
          Peacefully we glide.

Sweet is rest: the summer day is done,
          Gone the ardent sun.
All is still: no wind of twilight blows;
Shuts the evening like a crimson rose;
          Night comes like a nun.

Lift we loving voices, pure and clear,
          To the Father's ear;
Fragrant as the flowers the thoughts we raise
Up to heaven, while o'er the ocean ways
          Draws the darkness near.


## FLOWERS IN OCTOBER

The long black ledges are white with gulls,
    As if the breakers had left their foam;
With the dying daylight the wild wind lulls,
    And the scattered fishing-boats steer for home.

On the crag I sit, with the east before.
　The sun behind me is low in the sky;
Warm is its touch on the rocky shore;
　Sad the vast ocean spaces lie.

The cricket is hoarse in the faded grass;
　The low bush rustles so thin and sere;
Swift overhead the small birds pass,
　With cries that are lonely and sweet and clear.

The last chill asters their petals fold
　And gone is the morning-glory's bell,
But close in a loving hand I hold
　Long sprays of the scarlet pimpernel,

And thick at my feet are blossom and leaf,
　Blossoms rich red as the robes of kings;
Hardly they 're touched by the autumn's grief;
　Do they surmise what the winter brings?

I turn my eyes from the sweet, sad sky,
　From the foam-white gulls and the sails that
　　gleam,
To muse on the scattered flowers that lie
　Lost as yet in a summer dream.

O darlings, nursed by the salt sea-spray!
　O shapes of beauty so quaint and bright!

But for a little the frosts delay,
   Soon will be ended your brief delight.

Could I but succor you, every one,
   Spread wings of safety 'twixt harm and you;
Call from its southern travel the sun,
   Banish the snow from the arching blue!

It may not be, and the frosts must fall,
   The winter must reign in the summer's stead;
But, though you perish beyond recall,
   Ever I love you, alive or dead.


## WAIT

ARE the roses fallen, dear my child?
   Has the winter left us only thorns,
Sharp and shuddering stalks in tangles wild,
   Set with cruel teeth and iron horns?

Wait a little, fret not, and at last
   Beauty will the barren boughs again
Tenderly re-clothe, when snows are past,
   And the earth grows glad in sun and rain.

Never vex your heart nor tear your hands,
   Searching 'mid the thorns for vanished bliss;

For the soul that patience understands
  Needs no wisdom more divine than this:

Wait!  The sweet flowers of the coming spring
  Beautiful as those you mourn shall be.
Wait! for happy birds are sure to sing,
  While new roses bloom for you and me.


## KAREN

AT her low quaint wheel she sits to spin,
  Deftly drawing the long, light rolls
Of carded wool through her fingers thin,
  By the fireside at the Isles of Shoals.

She is not pretty, she is not young,
  Poor homesick Karen, who sits and spins,
Humming a song in her native tongue,
  That falters and stops, and again begins,

While her wheel flies fast, with its drowsy hum,
  And she makes a picture of pensive grace
As thoughts of her well-loved Norway come
  And deepen the shadows across her face.

Her collar is white as the drifted snow,
  And she spun and wove her blue gown fine

With those busy hands.   See, a flitting glow
 Makes her pale cheek burn and her dark eyes shine!

Left you a lover in that far land,
 O Karen sad, that you pine so long?
Would I could unravel and understand
 That sorrowful, sweet Norwegian song!

When the spring wind blew, the " America wind,"
 As your people call it, that bears away
Their youths and maidens a home to find
 In this distant country, could you not stay

And live in that dear Norway still,
 And let the emigrant crowd sail West
Without you?   Well, you have had your will.
 Why would you fly from your sheltering nest?

O homesick Karen, listen to me:
 You are not young, and you are not fair,
But Waldemar no one else can see,
 For he carries your image everywhere.

Is he too boyish a lover for you,
 With all his soul in his frank blue eyes?
Feign you unconsciousness?   Is it true
 You know not his heart in your calm hand lies?

Handsome and gentle and good is he;
  Loves you, Karen, better than life;
Do but consider him, can't you see
  What a happy woman would be his wife?

You won't be merry? You can't be glad?
  Still must you mourn for that home afar?
Well, here is an end of a hope I had,
  And I am sorry for Waldemar!


## A MUSSEL SHELL

WHY art thou colored like the evening sky
Sorrowing for sunset? Lovely dost thou lie,
Bared by the washing of the eager brine,
At the snow's motionless and wind-carved line.

Cold stretch the snows, cold throng the waves, the
          wind
Stings sharp, — an icy fire, a touch unkind, —
And sighs as if with passion of regret,
The while I mark thy tints of violet.

O beauty strange! O shape of perfect grace,
Whereon the lovely waves of color trace
The history of the years that passed thee by,
And touched thee with the pathos of the sky!

The sea shall crush thee; yea, the ponderous wave
Up the loose beach shall grind, and scoop thy grave,
Thou thought of God!   What more than thou am I?
Both transient as the sad wind's passing sigh.


## TRUST

SEE how the wind is hauling point by point to the
     south,
   By the boats in the little harbor, that swing to its
      lightest touch;
And the coasting craft emerge from the far-off river's
     mouth,
   And on the rocks the breakers relax their impotent
      clutch.


At last is the tempest ended, the bitter northeast
     appeased,
   And the world will soon be sparkling in clear white
      fire and dew,
And the sullen clouds melt swiftly, by the might of
     warm wind seized,
   And the heavens shine in splendor, where broadens
      the matchless blue.


Carol the birds in chorus; glitters the snow-white gull,
   Screaming loud in mid-air, slow-soaring high with
      delight;

And the rosebuds loosen their petals, the drenched
    flowers, sodden and dull,
  Break out into stars of purple and gold and crimson
    and white.

Where wert thou, Spirit of Beauty, while earth lay
    cold and dark,
  And the chill wind struck to our hearts, and the
    sky like an enemy scowled,
And we crept through the mists desponding, and never
    a glimmering spark
  Shot a ray through the gloom while the storm like
    a demon groveled and growled?

Where art thou, Heavenly Father, when thy world
    seems spoiled with sin,
  And darker far than thy tempest arises the smoke
    of doubt,
That blackens the sky of the soul? — for faith is hard
    to win:
  To our finite sight wrong triumphs and noble things
    die out,

While shapes of monstrous evil make fearful thy nights
    and days,
  And murder stalks unhindered, working its hideous
    will,

And innocence, gentleness, charity seem to forsake
    earth's ways,
  And in the hearts of thy creatures are madness and
    nameless ill.


Behind the cloud Thou waitest, hidden, yet very near,
  Infinite Spirit of Beauty, Infinite Power of Good!
At last Thou wilt scatter the vapors, and all things
    shall be clear,
  And evil shall vanish away like a mist by the wind
    pursued.


## MODJESKA

DEFT hands called Chopin's music from the keys.
  Silent she sat, her slender figure's poise
Flower-like and fine and full of lofty ease;
  She heard her Poland's most consummate voice
From power to pathos falter, sink and change;
  The music of her land, the wondrous high,
Utmost expression of its genius strange, —
  Incarnate sadness breathed in melody.
Silent and thrilled she sat, her lovely face
  Flushing and paling like a delicate rose
  Shaken by summer winds from its repose
Softly this way and that with tender grace,
  Now touched by sun, now into shadow turned, —
  While bright with kindred fire her deep eyes burned!

## SONG

O SWALLOW, sailing lightly
　　The crystal deeps of blue,
With flashing wings that brightly
　　Glitter the sunshine through,

What sayest thou, returning
　　From sunny lands and fair,
That summer roses burning
　　Shall light the fragrant air?

That merry days thou bringest,
　　And gone is winter's woe, —
Is this the song thou singest?
　　Gay prophet, is it so?

I know all beauties follow
　　Swift in thy shining track,
But to my heart, O swallow,
　　Canst thou bring summer back?

No shaft of sunshine glorious
　　Shall melt my winter snows,
No kiss of June victorious
　　Awake for me the rose!

## LARS

"Tell us a story of these isles," they said,
   The daughters of the West, whose eyes had seen
For the first time the circling sea, instead
   Of the blown prairie's waves of grassy green:

"Tell us of wreck and peril, storm and cold,
   Wild as the wildest."   Under summer stars,
With the slow moonrise at our back, I told
   The story of the young Norwegian, Lars.

That youth with the black eyebrows sharply drawn
   In strong curves, like some sea-bird's wings out-
      spread
O'er his dark eyes, is Lars, and this fair dawn
   Of womanhood, the maiden he will wed.

She loves him for the dangers he has past.
   Her rosy beauty glowed before his stern
And vigilant regard, until at last
   Her sweetness vanquished Lars the taciturn.

For he is ever quiet, strong, and wise;
   Wastes nothing, not a gesture nor a breath;
Forgets not, gazing in the maiden's eyes,
   A year ago it was not love, but death,

That clasped him, and can hardly learn as yet
    How to be merry, haunted by that pain
And terror, and remembering with regret
    The comrade he can never see again.

Out from the harbor on that winter day
    Sailed the two men to set their trawl together.
Down swept the sudden snow-squall o'er the bay,
    And hurled their slight boat onward like a feather.

They tossed they knew not whither, till at last
    Under the lighthouse cliff they found a lee,
And out the road-lines of the trawl they cast
    To moor her, if so happy they might be.

But quick the slender road-lines snapt in twain
    In the wild breakers, and once more they tossed
Adrift; and, watching from his misty pane,
    The lighthouse keeper muttered, "They are lost!"

Lifted the snow: night fell; swift cleared the sky;
    The air grew sharp as death with polar cold;
Raged the insensate gale, and flashing high
    In starlight keen the hissing billows rolled.

Driven before the wind's incessant scourge
    All night they fled, — one dead ere morning lay.
Lars saw his strange, drawn countenance emerge
    In the fierce sunrise light of that drear day,

And thought, "A little space and I shall be
    Even as he," and, gazing in despair
O'er the wide, weltering waste, no sign could see
    Of hope, or help, or comfort, anywhere.

Two hundred miles before the hurricane
    The dead and living drove across the sea.
The third day dawned.   His dim eyes saw again
    The vast green plain, breaking eternally

In ghastly waves.   But in the early light,
    On the horizon glittering like a star,
Fast growing, looming tall, with canvas white,
    Sailed his salvation southward from afar!

Down she bore, rushing o'er the hills of brine,
    Straight for his feeble signal.   As she past,
Out from the schooner's deck they flung a line,
    And o'er his head the open noose was cast.

Clutching with both his hands the bowline knot
    Caught at his throat, swift drawn through fire he
        seemed,
Whelmed in the icy sea, and he forgot
    Life, death, and all things, — yet he thought he
        dreamed

A dread voice cried, "We 've lost him!" and a sting
    Of anguish pierced his clouded senses through;

A moment more, and like a lifeless thing
   He lay among the eager, pitying crew.

Long time he swooned, while o'er the ocean vast
   The dead man tossed alone, they knew not where;
But youth and health triumphant were at last,
   And here is Lars, you see, and here the fair

Young snow-and-rose-bloom maiden he will wed.
   His face is kindly, though it seems so stern.
Death passed him by, and life begins instead,
   For Thora sweet and Lars the taciturn.

## SONG

A RUSHING of wings in the dawn,
   A flight of birds in the sky!
The darkness of night withdrawn,
   In an outburst of melody!

O birds through the heaven that soar
   With such tumult of jubilant song!
The shadows are flying before,
   For the rapture of life is strong,

And my spirit leaps to the light
   On the wings of its hope new-born,
And I follow your radiant flight
   Through the golden halls of morn!

## THORA

COME under my cloak, my darling!
　Thou little Norwegian maid!
Nor wind, nor rain, nor rolling sea
　Shall chill or make thee afraid.

Come close, little blue-eyed maiden,
　Nestle within my arm;
Though the lightning leaps and the thunder peals,
　We shall be safe from harm.

Swift from the dim horizon
　The dark sails scud for the land.
Look, how the rain-cloud drops its fringe
　About us on either hand!

And high from our plunging bowsprit
　Dashes the cold white spray,
And storm and tumult fill the air
　And trouble the summer day.

But thou fearest nothing, darling,
　Though the tempest mutter and brood,
Though the wild wind tosses thy bright brown locks,
　And flutters thy grass-green snood.

I kiss thy wise white forehead,
  While the thunder rolls so grand;
And I hold the curve of thy lovely cheek
  In the hollow of my hand;

And I watch the sky and the ocean,
  And study thy gentle face —
Its lines of sweetness and power,
  The type of thy strong Norse race.

And I wonder what thy life will be,
  Thou dear and charming child,
Who hast drifted so far across the world
  To a home so lone and wild.

Rude and rough and sad, perhaps;
  Anxious, and full of toil;
But I think no sorrow or hardship
  Thine inner peace can spoil.

For better than kingly fortunes
  Is the wealth that thou dost hold —
A nature perfectly balanced,
  A beauty of heart untold.

Thou wilt open the door of patience,
  When sorrow shall come and knock;
But to every evil, unworthy thing
  Wilt thou the gates fast lock.

So shall thy days be blessed,
   Whatever may be thy lot.
But what I am silently pondering
   Thou understandest not,

And liftest to me thy steadfast eyes,
   Calm as if Heaven looked through.
Do all the maidens in Norway
   Have eyes so clear and blue?

See, darling, where, in the distance,
   The cloud breaks up in the sky,
And lets a ray of sunshine fall
   Where our far-off islands lie!

White they gleam, and the sea grows bright,
   And silver shines the foam.
A little space, and our anchor drops
   In the haven of Love and Home!

## THE HAPPY BIRDS

ALL about the gable tall swift the swallows flit,
   Wheel and call and dart and, fluttering, chatter
      sweet;
All along the sloping, sunny eaves they perch and sit,
   Bright as lapis-lazuli, glittering in the heat.

O spirits of the summer, so dainty, delicate,
    Creatures born of sunshine and cheer and all de-
        light,
Pray you, but delay a moment, yet a little wait,
    Ere for southern lands again you spread your wings
        in flight!

Yet the August sun is hot, yet the days are long,
    Though the grass is over-ripe and the aster blows;
Still the silence echoes to the sparrow's quiet song,
    Still, though late, in thorny thickets lingers the
        wild rose.

Tarry yet a little, for after you have flown
    Lonely all the housetops and still the air will
        grow;
Where your cheerful voices rang autumn winds will
        moan;
    Presently we shall be dull with winter's weight of
        snow.

Oh! that we could follow you and cling to Summer's
        hand,
    Ye happy, happy birds, flying lightly through the
        sky!
Reach with you the rapture of some far, sunny land,
    Leave to Winter's bitterness our glad and gay good-
        by!

## SLUMBER SONG

Thou little child, with tender, clinging arms,
    Drop thy sweet head, my darling, down and rest
Upon my shoulder, rest with all thy charms;
    Be soothed and comforted, be loved and blessed.

Against thy silken, honey-colored hair
    I lean a loving cheek, a mute caress;
Close, close I gather thee and kiss thy fair
    White eyelids, sleep so softly doth oppress.

Dear little face, that lies in calm content
    Within the gracious hollow that God made
In every human shoulder, where He meant
    Some tired head for comfort should be laid!

Most like a heavy-folded rose thou art,
    In summer air reposing, warm and still.
Dream thy sweet dreams upon my quiet heart;
    I watch thy slumber; naught shall do thee ill.

## STARLIGHT

The chill, sad evening wind of winter blows
    Across the headland, bleak and bare and high,
Rustling the thin, dry grass that sparsely grows,
    And shivering whispers like a human sigh.

The sky is thick with stars that sparkle keen,
    And great Capella in the clear northeast
Rolls slowly up the cloudless heaven serene,
    And the stern uproar of the sea has ceased

A fleeting moment, and the earth seems dead —
    So still, so sad, so lonely, and so cold!
Snow-dust beneath me, and above my head
    Star-dust in blackness, like thick-sprinkled gold.

The stars of fire, the tiny stars of ice,
    The awful whirling worlds in space that wheel,
The dainty crystal's delicate device, —
    One hand has fashioned both — and I, who kneel

Here on this winter night, 'twixt stars and snow,
    As transient as a snowflake and as weak,
Yearning like all my fellow-men to know
    His hidden purpose that no voice may speak;

In silent awe I watch his worlds: I see
    Mighty Capella's signal, and I know
The steady beam of light that reaches me
    Left the great orb full seventy years ago.

A human lifetime!   Reason strives in vain
    To grasp at time and space, and evermore

Thought, weary grown and baffled, must again
   Retrace its slow steps to the humble door

Of wistful patience, there to watch and wait
   Devoutly, till at last Death's certain hand,
Imperious, opens wide the mystic gate
   Between us and the future He has planned.

Yea, Death alone.    But shall Death conquer all?
   Love fights and pleads in anguish of despair.
Sooner shall great Capella wavering fall
   Than any voice respond to his wild prayer.

And yet, what fire divine makes hope to glow
   Through the pale ashes of our earthly fate?
Immortal hope, above all joy, below
   All depths of pain wherein we strive and wait!

Dull is our sense; hearing we do not hear,
   And seeing see not; yet we vaguely feel
Somewhere is comfort in the darkness drear,
   And, hushing doubts and fears, we learn to kneel.

Starlight and silence!   Dumb are sky and sea;
   Silent as death the awful spaces lie;
Speechless the bitter wind blows over me,
   Sad as the breathing of a human sigh.

## SONG

HARK, how sweet the thrushes sing!
　　Hark, how clear the robins call!
Chorus of the happy spring,
　　Summer's madrigal!

Flood the world with joy and cheer,
　　O ye birds, and pour your song
Till the farthest distance hear
　　Notes so glad and strong!

Storm the earth with odors sweet,
　　O ye flowers, that blaze in light!
Crowd about June's shining feet,
　　All ye blossoms bright.

Shout, ye waters, to the sun!
　　Back are winter's fetters hurled;
Summer's glory is begun;
　　Beauty holds the world!

## REMONSTRANCE

"COME out and hear the birds sing! Oh, wherefore sit
　　you there
At the western window watching, dreamy-pale and
　　still and fair,

While the warm summer wind disparts your tresses'
    clustering gold ?
What is it on the dim sea line your eyes would fain
    behold ? "
" I seek a sail that never looms from out the purple
    haze
At rosy dawn, or fading eve, or in the noontide's
    blaze. "

" A sail ?   Lo, many a column of white canvas far and
    near !
All day they glide across the blue, appear and disap-
    pear;
See, how they crowd the offing, flocking from the sul-
    try South !
Why stirs a smile more sad than tears the patience of
    your mouth ? "
" They lean before the freshening breeze, they cross
    the ocean floor,
But the ship that brings me tidings of my love comes
    never more. "

" Come out into the garden where the crimson phloxes
    burn,
And every slender lily-stem upbears a lustrous urn;
A thousand greetings float to you from bud and bell
    and star,

Their sweetness freights the breathing wind; how
    beautiful they are!"
"Their brilliant color blinds me; I sicken at their
    breath;
The whisper of this mournful wind is sad to me as
    death."

"And must you sit so white and cold while all the
    world is bright?
Ah, come with me and see how all is brimming with
    delight!
On the beach the emerald breaker murmurs o'er the
    tawny sand;
The white spray from the rock is tossed, by melting
    rainbows spanned."
"Nay, mock me not! I have no heart for nature's
    happiness;
One sound alone my soul can fill, one shape my sight
    can bless."

"And are your fetters forged so fast, though you were
    free and strong,
By the old, mysterious madness, told in story and in
    song
Since burdened with the human race the world began
    to roll?
Can you not thrust the weight away, so heavy on your
    soul?"

"There is no power in earth or heaven such madness
      to destroy,
And I would not part with sorrow that is sweeter far
      than joy."

"Oh marvelous content, that from such still despair is
      born!
Nay, I would wrestle with my fate till love were slain
      with scorn!
O mournful Mariana!   I would never sit so pale,
Watching, with eyes grown dim with dreams, the
      coming of a sail!"
"Peace, peace!   How can you measure a depth you
      never knew?
My chains to me are dearer than your freedom is to
      you."


## MORNING SONG

WE launch our boat upon the sparkling sea,
    We dip our rhythmic oars with song and cheer;
Before our dancing prow the shadows flee,
    Behind us fast the fair coasts disappear.

So fade our childhood's shores.   Without regret
    We leave the safe, green, happy fields, and try
The vague, uncertain ocean, storm-beset,
    Nor see the tempests that before us lie.

Flushed with our hope the unknown future gleams,
    Freighted with blissful dreams our barque floats on,
And life a shining path of victory seems,
    Crowned with a golden peace when day is done.


## BEETHOVEN

IF God speaks anywhere, in any voice,
    To us, his creatures, surely here and now
    We hear Him, while the great chords seem to bow
Our heads, and all the symphony's breathless noise
    Breaks over us with challenge to our souls!
Beethoven's music! From the mountain peaks
    The strong, divine, compelling thunder rolls,
And, "Come up higher, come!" the words it speaks,
    "Out of your darkened valleys of despair,
Behold, I lift you upon mighty wings
    Into Hope's living, reconciling air!
Breathe, and forget your life's perpetual stings;
    Dream, — folded on the breast of Patience sweet,
    Some pulse of pitying love for you may beat!"


## SONG

WHAT good gift can I bring thee, O thou dearest!
    All joys to thee belong;
Thy praise from loving lips all day thou hearest,
    Sweeter than any song.

For thee the sun shines and the earth rejoices
    In fragrance, music, light;
The spring-time woos thee with a thousand voices,
    For thee her flowers are bright;
Youth crowns thee, and love waits upon thy splendor,
    Trembling beneath thine eyes;
The morning sky is yet serene and tender,
    Thy life before thee lies.
What shall I bring thee, O thou dearest, fairest!
    Thou holdest in thy hand
My heart as lightly as the rose thou wearest;
    Nor wilt thou understand
Thou art my sun, my rose, my day, my morrow,
    My lady proud and sweet!
I bring the treasure of a priceless sorrow,
    To lay before thy feet.


## WITH THE TIDE

Swift o'er the water my light yacht dances,
    Flying fast from the wind of the South;
Bright from her bowsprit the white foam glances,
    And straight we steer for the harbor's mouth.

The coast line dim from the haze emerges,
    With tender tints of the spring-time toned;
On silver beaches roll sparkling surges,
    And woods are green on the hills enthroned.

The sentinel lighthouses watch together,
  As the stately river we reach at last;
The robins sing in the blithe May weather,
  And the flood-tide bears us onward fast.

From bank to bank flows a chorus mellow
  Of rippling frogs and of singing birds;
The fields are starry with flowers of yellow,
  And green slopes pasture the lowing herds.

A lovely perfume blows softly over
  From apple-blossoms on either side,
From golden willow and budding clover,
  And many a garden of lowly pride.

And a lazy echo of glad cocks crowing
  From door-yards cosy rings far and near!
And the city's murmur is slowly growing
  From out the distance distinct and clear.

Over the river, so broadly flowing,
  Cottages look from the sheltering trees;
And out through the orchard, with blossoms snowing,
  Comes a brown-haired maiden from one of these.

She waves her hand as in friendly token,
  And watches my swift boat sailing on;
I answer her signal — no word is spoken,
  'T is but a moment, and she is gone.

And when, from the far-off town returning,
  Dropping down with the ebbing tide,
Seaward we sail, with the sunset burning
  O'er wastes of the ocean, lone and wide,

Again in the orchard her white hand lifted
  Shows like a waft of a sea-bird's wing,
While the rosy blossoms are o'er her drifted,
  And loud with rapture the robins sing.

I know her not and shall know her never,
  But ever I watch for that friendly sign;
And up or down with the stately river
  Her lovely greeting is always mine.

And her presence lends to the scene a glory,
  More beauty to blossom and stream and tree;
And back o'er the wastes of the ocean hoary
  Her gentle image I take with me.

## "THE SUNRISE NEVER FAILED US YET"

UPON the sadness of the sea
The sunset broods regretfully;
From the far lonely spaces, slow
Withdraws the wistful afterglow.

So out of life the splendor dies;
So darken all the happy skies;
So gathers twilight, cold and stern;
But overhead the planets burn;

And up the east another day
Shall chase the bitter dark away;
What though our eyes with tears be wet?
The sunrise never failed us yet.

The blush of dawn may yet restore
Our light and hope and joy once more.
Sad soul, take comfort, nor forget
That sunrise never failed us yet!

## ENTHRALLED

LIKE huge waves, petrified, against the sky,
    The solemn hills are heaved; by shadow kissed,
Or softly touched by delicate light they lie
    Melting in sapphire and in amethyst.

The thronging mountains, crowding all the scene,
    Are like the long swell of an angry sea,
Tremendous surging tumult that has been
    Smitten to awful silence suddenly.

The nearer slopes with autumn glory blaze,
    Garnet and ruby, topaz, amber, gold;

Up through the quiet air the thin smoke strays
   From many a lonely homestead, brown and old.

The scattered cattle graze in pastures bare,
   The brooks sing unconcerned beside the way,
Belated crickets chirp, while still and fair
   Dies into sunset peace the golden day.

And toward the valley, where the little town
   Beckons with twinkling lights, that gleam below
Like bright and friendly eyes, we loiter down
   And find our shelter and our fireside glow.

But while the gay hours pass with laugh and jest,
   And all is radiant warmth and joy once more,
My captured thought must wander out in quest
   Of that vast mountain picture, o'er and o'er;

Where underneath the black and star-sown arch
   Earth's ancient trouble speaks eternally;
And I must watch those mighty outlines march
   In silence, motionless, with none to see;

While from the north the night-wind sighing sweeps,
   And, sharp against the crystal sky relieved,
The tumult of forgotten ages sleeps
   Where like huge waves the solemn hills are heaved.

## SONG

ROLLS the long breaker in splendor, and glances,
    Leaping in light!
Sparkling and singing the swift ripple dances,
    Laughing and bright;
Up through the heaven the curlew is flying,
    Soaring so high!
Sweetly his wild notes are ringing, and dying,
    Lost in the sky.
Glitter the sails to the south-wind careening,
    White-winged and brave;
Bowing to breeze and to billow, and leaning
    Low o'er the wave.
Beautiful wind, with the touch of a lover
    Leading the hours,
Helping the winter-worn world to recover
    All its lost flowers,
Gladly I hear thy warm whisper of rapture,
    Sorrow is o'er!
Earth all her music and bloom shall recapture,
    Happy once more.

## TRANSITION

A CLASH of human tongues within
　　Made the bright room a dreary jail;
Dull webs of talk the idle spin
　　Turned all its glow and color pale.

Outside, the peaceful sunset sky
　　Was burning, deepening with the night;
One great star, glittering still and high,
　　Sent o'er the sea its track of light.

And wearily I spoke, and heard
　　An empty echo of reply,
Fretting like some imprisoned bird
　　That longs to break its cage and fly;

When suddenly the din seemed stilled,
　　Rarer the air so dense before;
A mystic rapture warmed and thrilled
　　My heart, and I was dull no more.

Joy stole to me with sweet surmise,
　　With sense of some unmeasured good;
There was no need to lift my eyes
　　To know who on the threshold stood,

More splendid than the brilliant night
That looked in at the window-pane,
Welcome as to parched fields the light,
Refreshing touch of summer rain!

She moved with recognition sweet,
She bowed with courtesy calm and kind,
As graceful as the waving wheat
That bends before the summer wind.

Swift sped the step of lagging time,
As if a breeze of morning blew;
Clear as the ring of Chaucer's rhyme
The vapid, idle talking grew!

I heard her rich tones sounding through
The many voices like a strain
Of lofty music, strong and true,
And perfect joy was mine again.

I did not seek her radiant face,
Bright as spring light when winter dies,
But warm across the crowded space
I felt the gaze of noble eyes;

And in that glorious look, at last,
I seemed like one with sins forgiven,
With all life's pain and sorrow passed,
Entering the open gates of heaven!

## LEVIATHAN

BETWIXT the bleak rock and the barren shore
  Rolled miles of hoary waves that hissed with frost,
And from the bitter north with sullen roar
  Swept the wild wind, and the wild water tossed.

In the cold sky, hard, pitiless, and drear,
  The sun dropped down; but ere the world grew
    gray,
A sweet, reluctant rose-tint, sad and clear,
  Stained icy crags and leagues of leaping spray.

Midway between the lone rock and the shore
  A fountain fair sprang skyward suddenly,
And sudden fell, and yet again once more
  The column rose, and sank into the sea.

Silent, ethereal, mystic, delicate,
  Flushed with delicious glow of fading rose,
It grew and vanished, like some genie great,
  Some wild, thin phantom, woven of winter snows.

'T was the foam-fountain of the mighty whale,
  Rising each time more far and faint and dim.
All his huge strength against the thundering gale
  He set; no hurricane could hinder him!

There came to me a gladness in the sight,
    A pleasure in the thought of life so strong,
Daring the elements, and making light
    Of winter's wrathful power of wreck and wrong.

I gloried in his triumph o'er the vast
    Blind rage of Nature.   All her awful force,
The terror of her tempest full she cast
    Against him, yet he kept his ponderous course.

For her worst fury he nor stayed nor turned.
    'T was joy to think in such tremendous play,
Through the sea's cruelty, all unconcerned,
    Leviathan pursued his placid way!


## TO A VIOLIN

WHAT wondrous power from heaven upon thee
    wrought?
What prisoned Ariel within thee broods?
Marvel of human skill and human thought,
    Light as a dry leaf in the winter woods!

Thou mystic thing, all beautiful!   What mind
    Conceived thee, what intelligence began
And out of chaos thy rare shape designed,
    Thou delicate and perfect work of man?

Across my hands thou liest mute and still;
　　Thou wilt not breathe to me thy secret fine;
Thy matchless tones the eager air shall thrill
　　To no entreaty or command of mine;

But comes thy master, lo! thou yieldest all:
　　Passion and pathos, rapture and despair;
To the soul's need thy searching voice doth call
　　In language exquisite beyond compare,

Till into speech articulate at last
　　Thou seem'st to break, and thy charmed listener
　　　　hears
Thee waking echoes of the vanished past,
　　Touching the source of gladness and of tears;

And with bowed head he lets the sweet wave roll
　　Across him, swayed by that weird power of thine,
And reverence and wonder fill his soul
　　That man's creation should be so divine.


## PHILOSOPHY

So soon the end must come,
　　Why waste in sighs our breath?
So soon our lips are dumb,
　　So swift comes death.

So brief the time to smile,
  Why darken we the air
With frowns and tears, the while
  We nurse despair?

Hold firm the suffering will
  And bravely thrust it back;
Fight with the powers of ill,
  The legions black.

Stand in the sunshine sweet
  And treasure every ray,
Nor seek with stubborn feet
  The darksome way.

Have courage! Keep good cheer!
  Our longest time is brief.
To those who hold you dear
  Bring no more grief.

But cherish blisses small,
  Grateful for least delight
That to your lot doth fall,
  However slight.

And lo! all hearts will bring
  Love, to make glad your days:
Blessings untold will spring
  About your ways.

So shall life bloom and shine,
 Lifted its pain above,
Crowned with this gift divine,
 The gift of Love.


## MEDRICK AND OSPREY

MEDRICK, waving wide wings low over the breeze-
 rippled bight;
 Osprey, soaring superb overhead in the fathomless
  blue,
Graceful and fearless and strong, do you thrill with
 the morning's delight
 Even as I? Brings the sunshine a message of beauty
  for you?


Oh the blithe breeze of the west, blowing sweet from
 the far-away land,
 Bowing the grass heavy-headed, thick crowding, so
  slender and proud!
Oh the warm sea sparkling over with waves by the
 swift wind fanned!
 Oh the wide sky crystal clear, with bright islands of
  delicate cloud!


Feel you the waking of life in the world locked long
 time in the frost,
 Beautiful birds, with the light flashing bright from
  your banner-like wings?

Osprey, soaring on high, in the depths of the sky half
    lost,
  Medrick, hovering low where the sandpiper's sweet
    note rings!

Nothing am I to you, a blot, perhaps, on the day;
  Naught do I add to your joy, but precious you are
    in my sight;
And you seem on your glad wings to lift me up into
    the ether away,
  And the morning divine is more radiant because of
    your glorious flight.


## ALONE

THE lilies clustered fair and tall;
I stood outside the garden wall;
I saw her light robe glimmering through
The fragrant evening's dusk and dew.

She stooped above the lilies pale;
Up the clear east the moon did sail;
I saw her bend her lovely head
O'er her rich roses blushing red.

Her slender hand the flowers caressed,
Her touch the unconscious blossoms blessed;

The rose against her perfumed palm
Leaned its soft cheek in blissful calm.

I would have given my soul to be
That rose she touched so tenderly!
I stood alone, outside the gate,
And knew that life was desolate.


## REVERIE

THE white reflection of the sloop's great sail
   Sleeps trembling on the tide;
In scarlet trim her crew lean o'er the rail,
   Lounging on either side.

Pale blue and streaked with pearl the waters lie
   And glitter in the heat;
The distance gathers purple bloom where sky
   And glimmering coast-line meet.

From the cove's curving rim of sandy gray
   The ebbing tide has drained,
Where, mournful, in the dusk of yesterday
   The curlew's voice complained.

Half lost in hot mirage the sails afar
   Lie dreaming, still and white;

No wave breaks, no wind breathes, the peace to mar;
    Summer is at its height.


How many thousand summers thus have shone
    Across the ocean waste,
Passing in swift succession, one by one,
    By the fierce winter chased!


The gray rocks blushing soft at dawn and eve,
    The green leaves at their feet,
The dreaming sails, the crying birds that grieve,
    Ever themselves repeat.


And yet how dear and how forever fair
    Is Nature's friendly face,
And how forever new and sweet and rare
    Each old familiar grace!


What matters it that she will sing and smile
    When we are dead and still?
Let us be happy in her beauty while
    Our hearts have power to thrill.


Let us rejoice in every moment bright,
    Grateful that it is ours;
Bask in her smiles with ever fresh delight,
    And gather all her flowers;

For presently we part: what will avail
　　Her rosy fires of dawn,
Her noontide pomps, to us, who fade and fail,
　　Our hands from hers withdrawn?


## HEART'S—EASE

SOUTHWARD still the sun is slanting day by day,
　　Skies that brim with gold and azure slowly change;
Beauty waxes cold and dim and cannot stay,
　　Into tone and tint steals something ill and strange.


Threat of evil finds its way to every ear,
　　Lurks in light and shade and sounds in every
　　　　breath;
From the pathless snow-fields comes a warning drear,
　　And the shuddering north-wind carries news of
　　　　death.


Stealthy step of Winter near and nearer draws:
　　Locking earth beneath him, terrible with might,
Strides he from the icy zone without a pause,
　　Swift and sure and fierce, with ready hand to smite.


Dearest, when without the door he threatening stands,
　　Having rendered desolate the fair green earth,
And sent her happy birds to sunnier lands,
　　And choked with sullen snows her summer mirth,

We shall sit together, you and I, once more,
    Warm and quiet, shut away from storm and cold;
We shall smile to hear him blustering at the door,
    While the room glows with the firelight's ruddy
        gold.

How safe my heart keeps every memory sweet,
    Holding still your picture, as you used to sit,
Ever lovely, full of grace from head to feet,
    With that heap of snowy wool I watched you
        knit;

With the lamplight falling on your cloudy hair —
    On the rich, loose bands of brown, so soft to touch;
On the silken knot of rose you used to wear,
    On the thoughtful little face I love so much.

You remember, when aloud I read to you,
    Sometimes silence intervened. You would not
        move,
But in your radiant cheek the blushes grew,
    For you knew I paused to gaze at you, my love!

Paused to realize my heaven, till with kind,
    Clear and questioning gray eyes you sought my face.
What a look! Its kindling glory struck me blind;
    'T was a splendor that illumined all the place.

What to us are Winter's blows and hate and wrath?
  And what matter that the green earth's bloom is
    fled?
There has been immortal summer in our path
  All the happy, happy years since we were wed.


## AUTUMN

ROUND and round the garden rushed a sudden blast,
  Crying, "Autumn! Autumn!" shuddering as it
    passed.
Dry poppy-head and larkspur-spike shrill whistled in
    the wind,
  Together whispering, "Autumn! and Winter is be-
    hind!"


Tossed the sumach pennons, green and gold and red;
  Flapped the awning scallops loudly overhead;
Swung the empty hammocks lightly to and fro;
  While the crickets simmered, chirruping below.


Keen the star of evening hung glittering in the sky,
  Red the west was burning, deepening silently;
Summer constellations slow wheeling out of sight,
  Great Orion shining clear upon the face of night.


Sadly sang the ocean, sighing in the dark;
  Far away the lighthouse lit a sudden spark;

Black against the sunset sails were gliding past;
  Earth and sea and sky were saying, "Autumn 's here
    at last!"

Soon will snow be flying, soon will tempests roar,
  Soon the freezing north will lash us bitter as before;
I heard the waters whisper, I heard the winds com-
    plain,
  But sweet, reluctant Summer I knew would come
    again.

## SONG

Love, art thou weary with the sultry day?
  Fain would I be the cool and delicate air
About the whiteness of thy brow to play,
  And softly, lightly stir thy cloudy hair.

Upon thy head doth the fierce winter smite,
  And shudderest thou in darkness cold to be?
I would I were the coming of the light,
  Shelter, and radiant warmth to comfort thee.

I would be fire and fragrance, light and air,
  All gracious things that serve thee at thy need;
Music, to lift thy heart above all care;
  The wise and charming book that thou dost read.

There is no power that cheers and blesses thee
But I do envy it, beneath the sun!
Thy health, thy rest, thy refuge I would be;
Thy heaven on earth, thine every good in one.


## SUBMISSION

THE sparrow sits and sings, and sings;
Softly the sunset's lingering light
Lies rosy over rock and turf,
And reddens where the restless surf
Tosses on high its plumes of white.

Gently and clear the sparrow sings,
While twilight steals across the sea,
And still and bright the evening-star
Twinkles above the golden bar
That in the west lies quietly.

Oh, steadfastly the sparrow sings,
And sweet the sound; and sweet the touch
Of wooing winds; and sweet the sight
Of happy Nature's deep delight
In her fair spring, desired so much!

But while so clear the sparrow sings
A cry of death is in my ear;

The crashing of the riven wreck,
  Breakers that sweep the shuddering deck,
And sounds of agony and fear.

How is it that the birds can sing?
  Life is so full of bitter pain;
    Hearts are so wrung with hopeless grief;
    Woe is so long and joy so brief;
  Nor shall the lost return again.

Though rapturously the sparrow sings,
  No bliss of Nature can restore
    The friends whose hands I clasped so warm,
    Sweet souls that through the night and storm
  Fled from the earth for evermore.

Yet still the sparrow sits and sings,
  Till longing, mourning, sorrowing love,
    Groping to find what hope may be
    Within death's awful mystery,
  Reaches its empty arms above;

And listening, while the sparrow sings,
  And soft the evening shadows fall,
    Sees, through the crowding tears that blind,
    A little light, and seems to find
  And clasp God's hand, who wrought it all.

## SONG

I WORE your roses yesterday:
  About this light robe's folds of white,
Wherein their gathered sweetness lay,
  Still clings their perfume of delight.

And all in vain the warm wind sweeps
  These airy folds like vapor fine,
Among them still the odor sleeps,
  And haunts me with a dream divine.

So to my heart your memory clings,
  So sweet, so rich, so delicate:
Eternal summer-time it brings,
  Defying all the storms of fate;

A power to turn the darkness bright,
  Till life with matchless beauty glows;
Each moment touched with tender light,
  And every thought of you a rose!

## SPRING AGAIN

I STOOD on the height in the stillness
  And the planet's outline scanned,
And half was drawn with the line of sea
  And half with the far blue land.

With wings that caught the sunshine
   In the crystal deeps of the sky,
Like shapes of dreams, the gleaming gulls
   Went slowly floating by.

Below me the boats in the harbor
   Lay still, with their white sails furled;
Sighing away into silence,
   The breeze died off the world.

On the weather-worn, ancient ledges
   Peaceful the calm light slept;
And the chilly shadows, lengthening,
   Slow to the eastward crept.

The snow still lay in the hollows,
   And where the salt waves met
The iron rock, all ghastly white
   The thick ice glimmered yet.

But the smile of the sun was kinder,
   The touch of the air was sweet;
The pulse of the cruel ocean seemed
   Like a human heart to beat.

Frost-locked, storm-beaten, and lonely,
   In the midst of the wintry main,

Our bleak rock yet the tidings heard:
"There shall be spring again!"

Worth all the waiting and watching,
  The woe that the winter wrought,
Was the passion of gratitude that shook
  My soul at the blissful thought!

Soft rain and flowers and sunshine,
  Sweet winds and brooding skies,
Quick-flitting birds to fill the air
  With clear, delicious cries;

And the warm sea's mellow murmur
  Resounding day and night;
A thousand shapes and tints and tones
  Of manifold delight,

Nearer and ever nearer
  Drawing with every day!
But a little longer to wait and watch
  'Neath skies so cold and gray,

And hushed is the roar of the bitter north
  Before the might of the Spring,
And up the frozen slope of the world
  Climbs Summer, triumphing.

## SONNET

As happy dwellers by the seaside hear
  In every pause the sea's mysterious sound,
  The infinite murmur, solemn and profound,
Incessant, filling all the atmosphere,
  Even so I hear you, for you do surround
My newly-waking life, and break for aye
  About the viewless shores, till they resound
With echoes of God's greatness night and day.
Refreshed and glad I feel the full flood-tide
  Fill every inlet of my waiting soul;
  Long-striving, eager hope, beyond control,
For help and strength at last is satisfied;
  And you exalt me, like the sounding sea,
  With ceaseless whispers of eternity.

## SONG

ABOVE in her chamber her voice I hear
      Singing so clear;
Among her flowers I stand and wait,
Dreaming I lean on the garden gate,
      In joy and fear.

Softly the light robes she doth wear
      Sweep down the stair;

O eager heart, less wildly beat, —
I shall behold her, stately, sweet,
　　All good and fair!

Nearer, her voice!　In a moment more
　　Through the open door
Come grace and beauty and all delight
The round world holds to my dazzled sight,
　　The threshold o'er!

She holds me mute with her beaming eyes
　　Full of bright surprise;
Still grow the pulses her coming shook,
In the gentle might of her golden look
　　My heaven lies!


## FOREBODING

CRICKET, why wilt thou crush me with thy cry?
How can such light sound weigh so heavily!
Behold the grass is sere, the cold dews fall,
The world grows empty — yes, I know it all,
　　　　The knell of joy I hear.

Oh, long ago the swallows hence have flown,
And sadly sings the sea in undertone;
The wild vine crimsons o'er the rough gray stone;
The stars of winter rise, the cool winds moan;
　　　　Fast wanes the golden year.

O cricket, cease thy sorrowful refrain.
This summer's glory comes not back again,
But others wait with flowers and sun and rain;
Why wakest thou this haunting sense of pain,
    Of loss, regret, and fear?

Clear sounds thy note above the waves' low sigh,
Clear through the breathing wind that wanders by,
Clear through the rustle of dry grasses tall;
Thou chantest, "Joy is dead!" I know it all,
    The winter's woe is near.

## HOMAGE

NAY, comrade, 't is a weary path we tread
 Through this world's desert spaces, dull and dry,
And long ago died out youth's morning-red,
 And low the sunset fires before us lie:

And you are worn, though brave the face you wear.
 Forbear the deprecating gesture, take
The honest admiration that I bear
 Your genius, and be mute, for friendship's sake.

Up to your lips I lift a generous wine,
 Pure, perfumed, potent, living, sparkling bright;
A deep cup, brimming with a draught divine;
 Drink, then, and be refreshed with my delight.

It gladdens you?   You know the gift sincere?
   You dreamed not life yet held a thing so sweet?
Nay, noble friend, your thanks I will not hear,
   But I shall cast my roses at your feet,

And go my way rejoicing that 't is I
   Who recognize, acknowledge, judge you best,
Proud that a star so steadfast lights the sky,
   And in the power of blessing you most blest.


## DISCONTENT

   THERE is no day so dark
But through the murk some ray of hope may steal.
Some blessed touch from Heaven that we might feel,
   If we but chose to mark.

   We shut the portals fast,
And turn the key and let no sunshine in;
Yet to the worst despair that comes through sin
   God's light shall reach at last.

   We slight our daily joy,
Make much of our vexations, thickly set
Our path with thorns of discontent, and fret
   At our fine gold's alloy,

   Till bounteous Heaven might frown
At such ingratitude, and, turning, lay

On our impatience burdens that would weigh
    Our aching shoulders down.

    We shed too many tears,
And sigh too sore, and yield us up to woe,
As if God had not planned the way we go
    And counted out our years.

    Can we not be content,
And lift our foreheads from the ignoble dust
Of these complaining lives, and wait with trust,
    Fulfilling Heaven's intent?

    Must we have wealth and power,
Fame, beauty, all things ordered to our mind
Nay, all these things leave happiness behind!
    Accept the sun and shower,

    The humble joys that bless,
Appealing to indifferent hearts and cold
With delicate touch, striving to reach and hold
    Our hidden consciousness;

    And see how everywhere
Love comforts, strengthens, helps, and saves us all;
What opportunities of good befall
    To make life sweet and fair!

## ALREADY

ALREADY the dandelions
   Are changed into vanishing ghosts;
Already the tall ripe grasses
   Are standing in serried hosts,

Bowing with stately gesture
   Whenever the warm winds blow,
Like the spear-heads of an army
   Charging against the foe.

Already the nestling sparrows
   Are clothed in a mist of gray,
And under the breast of the swallow
   The warm eggs stir to-day.

Already the cricket is busy
   With hints of soberer days,
And the goldenrod lights slowly
   Its torch for the autumn blaze.

O brief, bright smile of summer!
   O days divine and dear!
The voices of winter's sorrow
   Already we can hear.

And we know that the frosts will find us,
And the smiling skies grow rude,
While we look in the face of Beauty,
And worship her every mood.


## GUESTS

SUNFLOWER tall and hollyhock, that wave in the wind
together,
Cornflower, poppy, and marigold, blossoming fair
and fine,
Delicate sweet-peas, glowing bright in the quiet autumn
weather,
While over the fence, on fire with bloom, climbs
the nasturtium vine!


Quaint little wilderness of flowers, straggling hither
and thither —
Morning-glories tangled about the larkspur gone to
seed,
Scarlet runners that burst all bounds, and wander,
heaven knows whither,
And lilac spikes of bergamot, as thick as any weed.


And oh, the bees and the butterflies, the humming-
birds and sparrows,
That over the garden waver and chirp and flutter
the livelong day!

Humming-birds, that dart in the sun like green and
golden arrows,
Butterflies like loosened flowers blown off by the
wind in play.

Look at the red nasturtium flower, drooping, bending,
and swaying;
Out the gold-banded humble-bee breaks and goes
booming anew!
Hark, what the sweet-voiced fledgeling sparrows low
to themselves are saying,
Pecking my golden oats where the cornflowers
gleam so blue!

Welcome, a thousand times welcome, ye dear and deli-
cate neighbors —
Bird and bee and butterfly, and humming-bird fairy
fine!
Proud am I to offer you a field for your graceful
labors;
All the honey and all the seeds are yours in this
garden of mine.

I sit on the doorstep and watch you. Beyond lies
the infinite ocean,
Sparkling, shimmering, whispering, rocking itself to
rest;

And the world is full of perfume and color and beauti-
ful motion,
And each new hour of this sweet day the happiest
seems and best.

## MUTATION

ABOUT your window's happy height
The roses wove their airy screen:
More radiant than the blossoms bright
Looked your fair face between.

The glowing summer sunshine laid
Its touch on field and flower and tree;
But 't was your golden smile that made
The warmth that gladdened me.

The summer withered from the land,
The vision from the window passed:
Blank Sorrow looked at me; her hand
Sought mine and clasped it fast.

The bitter wind blows keen and drear,
Stinging with winter's flouts and scorns,
And where the roses breathed I hear
The rattling of the thorns.

## FAREWELL

THE crimson sunset faded into gray;
  Upon the murmurous sea the twilight fell;
The last warm breath of the delicious day
    Passed with a mute farewell.

Above my head, in the soft purple sky,
  A wild note sounded like a shrill-voiced bell;
Three gulls met, wheeled, and parted with a cry
    That seemed to say, "Farewell!"

I watched them: one sailed east, and one soared west,
  And one went floating south; while like a knell
That mournful cry the empty sky possessed,
    "Farewell, farewell, farewell!"

"Farewell!" I thought, it is the earth's one speech;
  All human voices the sad chorus swell;
Though mighty Love to heaven's high gate may reach,
    Yet must he say, "Farewell!"

The rolling world is girdled with the sound,
  Perpetually breathed from all who dwell
Upon its bosom, for no place is found
    Where is not heard, "Farewell!"

"Farewell, farewell!" — from wave to wave 't is
    tossed,
From wind to wind: earth has one tale to tell;
All other sounds are dulled and drowned and lost
    In this one cry, "Farewell!"


# DOUBT

THE wild rose blooms for the sun of June,
    The tide ebbs slowly out;
I hear in the dreamy afternoon
    The far-off fisher's shout.

The sand lies gray and the sea leaps blue,
    The tide ebbs slowly out;
O lover mine, who called to you,
    That you left me here to doubt?

The white gull's wing sweeps the whiter foam,
    The tide ebbs slowly out;
'T is not your white sail, yearning home
    To put my fears to rout!

The rose may blush and the sun may shine,
    The tide ebbs slowly out;
The world is good if you are mine,
    Ashes and dust without!

## SUNSET SONG

FAR off against the solemn sky
  Black lie the city's towers;
Before me rustles, dim and dry,
  My field of golden flowers.

How thin the wind's cool whisper draws
  Through withered leaf and stalk!
Is this the breeze that once would pause
  With blossoms bright to talk?

Dark lies the land in twilight sad,
  No bird sings in its bowers;
Where is the glory once that clad
  My field of golden flowers?

The distant city rings its bells,
  Like memory's tender chime;
O sweet, sweet bells, ye speak farewells
  To life's enchanted prime!

Dark lies the land in twilight cold,
  Gone are the sumptuous hours;
The city sleeps, and shadows fold
  My field of golden flowers.

## "LOVE SHALL SAVE US ALL"

O Pilgrim, comes the night so fast?
   Let not the dark thy heart appall,
Though loom the shadows vague and vast,
   For Love shall save us all.

There is no hope but this to see
   Through tears that gather fast and fall;
Too great to perish Love must be,
   And Love shall save us all.

Have patience with our loss and pain,
   Our troubled space of days so small;
We shall not reach our arms in vain,
   For Love shall save us all.

O Pilgrim, but a moment wait,
   And we shall hear our darlings call
Beyond death's mute and awful gate,
   And Love shall save us all!

## THE CRUISE OF THE MYSTERY

The children wandered up and down,
   Seeking for driftwood o'er the sand;
The elder tugged at granny's gown,
   And pointed with his little hand.

"Look! look!" he cried, "at yonder ship
　　That sails so fast and looms so tall!"
She turned, and let her basket slip,
　　And all her gathered treasure fall.

"Nay, granny, why are you so pale?
　　Where *is* the ship we saw but now?"
"Oh, child, it was no mortal sail!
　　It came and went, I know not how.

"But ill winds fill that canvas white
　　That blow no good to you and me.
Oh, woe for us who saw the sight
　　That evil bodes to all who see!"

They pressed about her, all afraid:
　　"Oh, tell us, granny, what was she?"
"A ship's unhappy ghost," she said,
　　"The awful ship, the Mystery."

"But tell us, tell us!"　"Quiet be!"
　　She said.　"Sit close and listen well,
For what befell the Mystery
　　It is a fearful thing to tell!"

———

She was a slave-ship long ago.
　　Year after year across the sea

She made a trade of human woe,
  And carried freights of misery.

One voyage, when from the tropic coast
  Laden with dusky forms she came, —
A wretched and despairing host, —
  Beneath the fierce sun's breathless flame

Sprang, like a wild beast from its lair,
  The fury of the hurricane,
And sent the great ship reeling bare
  Across the roaring ocean plain.

Then terror seized the piteous crowd:
  With many an oath and cruel blow
The captain drove them, shrieking loud,
  Into the pitch-black hold below.

Shouting, "Make fast the hatchways tight!"
  He cursed them: "Let them live or die,
They 'll trouble us no more to-night!"
  The crew obeyed him sullenly.

Has hell such torment as they knew?
  Like herded cattle packed they lay,
Till morning showed a streak of blue
  Breaking the sky's thick pall of gray.

"Off with the hatchways, men!"   No sound!
    What sound should rise from out a grave?
The silence shook with dread profound
    The heart of every seaman brave.

"Quick!   Drag them up," the captain said,
    "And pitch the dead into the sea!"
The sea was peopled with the dead,
    With wide eyes staring fearfully.

From weltering wave to wave they tossed.
    Two hundred corpses, stiff and stark,
At last were in the distance lost,
    A banquet for the wandering shark.

Oh, sweetly the relenting day
    Changed, till the storm had left no trace,
And the whole awful ocean lay
    As tranquil as an infant's face.

Abaft the wind hauled fair and fine,
    Lightly the ship sped on her way;
Her sharp bows crushed the yielding brine
    Into a diamond dust of spray.

But up and down the decks her crew
    Shook their rough heads, and eyed askance,
With doubt and hate that ever grew,
    The captain's brutal countenance,

As slow he paced with frown as black
    As night.    At last, with sudden shout,
He turned.    "'Bout ship!    We will go back
    And fetch another cargo out!"

They put the ship about again;
    His will was law, they could not choose.
They strove to change her course in vain:
    Down fell the wind, the sails hung loose,

And from the far horizon dim
    An oily calm crept silently
Over the sea from rim to rim;
    Still as if anchored fast lay she.

The sun set red, the moon shone white,
    On idle canvas drooping drear;
Through the vast, solemn hush of night
    What is it that the sailors hear?

Now do they sleep — and do they dream?
    Was that the wind's foreboding moan?
From stem to stern her every beam
    Quivered with one unearthly groan!

Leaped to his feet then every man,
    And shuddered, clinging to his mate;
And sunburned cheeks grew pale and wan,
    Blanched with that thrill of terror great.

The captain waked, and angrily
  Sprang to the deck, and cursing spoke.
"What devil's trick is this?" cried he.
  No answer the scared silence broke.

But quietly the moonlight clear
  Sent o'er the waves its pallid glow:
What stirred the water far and near,
  With stealthy motion swimming slow?

With measured strokes those swimmers dread
  From every side came gathering fast;
The sea was peopled with the dead
  That to its cruel deeps were cast!

And coiling, curling, crawling on,
  The phantom troop pressed nigh and nigher,
And every dusky body shone
  Outlined in phosphorescent fire.

They gained the ship, they climbed the shrouds,
  They swarmed from keel to topmast high;
Now here, now there, like filmy clouds
  Without a sound they flickered by.

And where the captain stood aghast,
  With hollow, mocking eyes they came,

And bound him fast unto the mast
  With ghostly ropes that bit like flame.


Like maniacs shrieked the startled crew!
  They loosed the boats, they leaped within;
Before their oars the water flew;
  They pulled as if some race to win.


With spectral light all gleaming bright
  The Mystery in the distance lay;
Away from that accursed sight
  They fled until the break of day.


And they were rescued, but the ship,
  The awful ship, the Mystery,
Her captain in the dead men's grip, —
  Never to any port came she;


But up and down the roaring seas
  For ever and for aye she sails,
In calm or storm, against the breeze,
  Unshaken by the wildest gales.


And wheresoe'er her form appears
  Come trouble and disaster sore,
And she has sailed a hundred years,
  And she will sail for evermore.

## SCHUMANN'S SONATA IN A MINOR

### (MIT LEIDENSCHAFTLICHEM AUSDRUCK)

THE quiet room, the flowers, the perfumed calm,
    The slender crystal vase, where all aflame
The scarlet poppies stand erect and tall,
    Color that burns as if no frost could tame,
The shaded lamplight glowing over all,
    The summer night a dream of warmth and balm.

Outbreaks at once the golden melody,
    "With passionate expression!"   Ah, from whence
Comes the enchantment of this potent spell,
    This charm that takes us captive, soul and sense?
The sacred power of music, who shall tell,
    Who find the secret of its mastery?

Lo, in the keen vibration of the air
    Pierced by the sweetness of the violin,
Shaken by thrilling chords and searching notes
    That flood the ivory keys, the flowers begin
To tremble; 't is as if some spirit floats
    And breathes upon their beauty unaware.

The stately poppies, proud in stillness, stand
    In silken splendor of superb attire:

Stricken with arrows of melodious sound,
  Their loosened petals fall like flakes of fire;
With waves of music overwhelmed and drowned,
  Solemnly drop their flames on either hand.

So the rich moment dies, and what is left?
  Only a memory sweet, to shut between
Some poem's silent leaves, to find again,
  Perhaps, when winter blasts are howling keen,
And summer's loveliness is spoiled and slain,
  And all the world of light and bloom bereft.

But winter cannot rob the music so!
  Nor time nor fate its subtle power destroy
To bring again the summer's dear caress,
  To wake the heart to youth's unreasoning joy, —
Sound, color, perfume, love, to warm and bless,
  And airs of balm from Paradise that blow.


## BECAUSE OF THEE

My life has grown so dear to me
      Because of thee!
My maiden with the eyes demure,
And quiet mouth, and forehead pure,
Joy makes a summer in my heart
      Because thou art!

The very winds melodious be
Because of thee!
The rose is sweeter for thy sake,
The waves in softer music break,
On brighter wings the swallows dart,
Because thou art!

My sky is swept of shadows free
Because of thee!
Sorrow and care have lost their sting,
The blossoms glow, the linnets sing,
All things in my delight have part,
Because thou art!

## FLOWERS FOR THE BRAVE

### (DECORATION DAY, 1883)

HERE bring your purple and gold,
Glory of color and scent;
Scarlet of tulips bold,
Buds blue as the firmament.

Hushed is the sound of the fife
And the bugle piping clear.
The vivid and delicate life
In the soul of the youthful year

We bring to the quiet dead,
   With a gentle and tempered grief:
O'er the mounds so mute we shed
   The beauty of blossom and leaf.

The flashing swords that were drawn,
   No rust shall their fame destroy!
Boughs rosy as rifts of dawn,
   Like the blush on the cheek of joy,

Rich fires of the gardens and meads
   We kindle, these hearts above!
What splendor can match their deeds?
   What sweetness can match our love?


## EXPOSTULATION

Tears in those eyes of blue!
Sparks of fiery dew,
Scornful lightnings that flash
'Twixt dusky lash and lash!
Never from sorrow grew
That rain in my heaven of blue.

Full of disdain are you,
Scorn for these fetters new.
Sweet, you were free too long!

Love is a master strong,
Hard are the words but true,
None may his chain undo.

Nay! Let your heart shine through
And soften those eyes of blue!
Glide from your chilly height,
Banish your anger bright;
Fairest, be gentlest, too,
Fate is too mighty for you!


## PERSISTENCE

SKELETON schooner, looming strange on the far hori-
    zon's rim,
Wasted and blurred by the bitter cold, all ghastly and
    pallid and dim,
Whither goest thou, stiff and stark? What harbor
    locked in the frost
Steerest thou for, through the freezing spray by the
    hissing breakers tossed?

Wherefore strivest thou, fighting still to plough thy
    perilous way
Against the might of the fierce northwest so woefully,
    night and day?

Turn thee and spread thy wings so white, and fly to
the tropic seas,
Till the clogging ice that loads thee now dissolves in a
torrid breeze;

Till the blazing sun shall melt the tar in every rope
and seam;
Till thy frozen keel warm tides shall rock in a languid,
lovely dream;
Till thou liest lapped in perfumes sweet in some palm-
girdled bay,
Anchored in peace, to rest at last, for many a golden
day.

What cheer can be in thy dreadful toil, what hope in
the raging deep?
What joy from out their troubled voyage can thy worn
seamen reap?
Loosen thy close-reefed canvas, then, fling wide thy
pinions white,
Leap the long billows, swiftly sail into the south's
delight!

Steadfast she steers to the bitter north along the hori-
zon's rim,
Wasted and blurred by the cruel cold, dull, ghostly,
and pallid, and dim;

For grand are the will and courage of man, and still
    she must keep her course,
And though she perish still must fight against nature's
    terrible force.

## S. E.

SHE passes up and down life's various ways
    With noiseless footfall and with serious air:
Within the circle of her quiet days
    She takes of sorrow and of joy her share.
In her bright home, like some rare jewel set,
    The lustre of her beauty lives and glows,
With all the fragrance of the violet,
    And all the radiant splendor of the rose.
As simple and unconscious as a flower,
    And crowned with womanhood's most subtle charm,
She blesses her sweet realm with gentle power,
    And keeps her hearth-fires burning clear and warm.
To know her is to love her.    Every year
Makes her more precious and more wise and dear.

## POOR LISETTE

SADLY the quails in the cornland pipe,
Yellow the harvest is bending ripe,
Gayly the children each other greet,
Wandering down through the village street.

By her garden gate leans poor Lisette.
"Her lover," they whisper, "comes not yet."
She looks afar to the edge of the sky,
Where blue and misty the mountains lie.

What sudden echoes of fife and drum
Down the long, dim, winding valley come!
Oh, bring they news for the poor Lisette,
Rapture at last, or a life's regret?

High ring the bugle notes so sweet,
Nearer the rhythmic tramp of feet, —
What tempest rushes to clasp Lisette,
With lips so warm and with eyes so wet!

She is safe in her lover's arms at last;
A dreary dream is the wretched past;
The music of joy in her glad heart plays,
And morning dawns in her radiant face:

While clearly the quails in the cornland pipe,
And silent the harvest is bending ripe,
And the children shout to the fife and drum
That pain is over and peace is come.

## TO J. G. W.

ON HIS SEVENTY-FIFTH BIRTHDAY

WHAT is there left, I wonder,
  To give thee on this glad day?
Vainly I muse and ponder;
  What is there left to say?

There is winter abroad, and snow,
  And winds that are chill and drear
Over the sad earth blow,
  Like the sighs of the dying year.

But the land thou lovest is warm
  At heart with the love of thee,
And breaks into bloom and charm
  And fragrance, that thou mayest see.

Violet, laurel, and rose,
  They are laid before thy feet,
And the red rose deeper glows
  At a fate so proud and sweet.

Gifts and greeting and blessing,
  Honor and praise, are thine;
There 's naught left worth expressing
  By any word or sign!

So, like the rest, I offer
The gift all gifts above
That heaven or earth can proffer, —
Deep, gentle, grateful love.

## IN TUSCANY

Down San Miniato in the afternoon
Slowly we drove through still and golden air.
'T was winter, but the day was soft as June;
Florence was spread beneath us, passing fair.

The matchless city!  Set about with flowers,
Peaceful along her Arno's banks she lay;
Her treasured splendors, roofs and domes and towers,
In tender light of the Italian day.

Sweet breathed the roses, glowing far and wide,
Pink, gold, and crimson; dark in stately gloom
Stood the thick cypresses; on every side
The laurestinus, rich with creamy bloom.

And exquisite, pale, sharp-leaved olives grew
In moonlight colors, silver-green and gray,
While, lifting their proud heads high in the blue,
Sprang the superb stone-pines beside the way.

Oh, wonderful, I thought, beyond compare!
   And hushed with pleasure silent sat and gazed,
When lo! a child's voice, and I grew aware
   Of loveliness that left me all amazed.

A little beggar girl, that leaping came
   Forth from the roadside, reaching out her hand,
And dancing like a bright and buoyant flame,
   Besought us in the music of her land.

Her eyes were like a midnight full of stars
   Below the dazzling beauty of her brows,
Her dusky hair dark as the cloud that bars
   The moon in troubled skies when tempests rouse;

A mouth where lightning-sweet the sudden smile
   Came, went and came, and flashed into my face,
And caught my heart, as, holding fast the while
   The carriage edge, she ran with rapid grace.

Who could withstand her pleading, who resist
   The magic of those love-compelling eyes,
Those lips the red pomegranate flowers had kissed,
   The voice that charmed like woven melodies!

Not we! Surely, I thought, imperial blood,
   Some priceless current from a kingly line,

Ran royal in her veins, — a sunny flood
That marked her with its fine, mysterious sign.

She was not born to ask, but to command;
She seemed to crown the wonder of the day,
The perfect blossom of that glorious land,
While her sweet "Grazie!" followed on our way,

As down 'mid olive, cypress, stately pine,
Among the roses in a dream we passed,
Through glamour of the time and place divine,
Till Arno's quiet banks were reached at last,

And pleasant rest.   'T is years since those fair hours,
But their rich memories live, their sun and shade,
Beautiful Florence set about with flowers,
And San Miniato's peerless beggar maid.


## GOOD–BY, SWEET DAY

### FOR MUSIC

Good-by, sweet day, good-by!
I have so loved thee, but I cannot hold thee.
Departing like a dream, the shadows fold thee;
Slowly thy perfect beauty fades away:
Good-by, sweet day!

Good-by, sweet day, good-by!
Dear were thy golden hours of tranquil splendor,
Sadly thou yieldest to the evening tender
Who wert so fair from thy first morning ray;
Good-by, sweet day!

Good-by, sweet day, good-by!
Thy glow and charm, thy smiles and tones and glances,
Vanish at last, and solemn night advances;
Ah, couldst thou yet a little longer stay!
Good-by, sweet day!

Good-by, sweet day, good-by!
All thy rich gifts my grateful heart remembers,
The while I watch thy sunset's smouldering embers
Die in the west beneath the twilight gray.
Good-by, sweet day!


## IN AUTUMN

THE aster by the brook is dead,
   And quenched the goldenrod's brief fire;
The maple's last red leaf is shed,
   And dumb the birds' sweet choir.

'T is life's November, too.   How swift
   The narrowing days speed, one by one!

How pale the waning sunbeams sift
　　Through clouds of gray and dun!

And as we lose our wistful hold
　　On warmth and loveliness and youth,
And shudder at the dark and cold,
　　Our souls cry out for Truth.

No more mirage, O Heavenly Powers,
　　To mock our sight with shows so fair!
We question of the solemn hours
　　That lead us swiftly — "Where?"

We hunger for our lost — in vain!
　　We lift our close-clasped hands above,
And pray God's pity on our pain,
　　And trust the Eternal Love.


## WEST–WIND

THE barley bows from the west
　　Before the delicate breeze
That many a sail caressed
　　As it swept the sapphire seas.

It has found the garden sweet,
　　And the poppy's cup it sways;

Bends the golden ears of wheat;
   And its dreamy touch it lays

On the heavy mignonette,
   Stealing soft its odors fine,
On the pansies dewy yet,
   On the phloxes red as wine.

Where the honeysuckle sweet
   Storms the sunny porch with flowers,
Like a tempest of delight
   Shaking fragrance down in showers,

It touches with airy grace
   Each clustering, perfumed spray,
Clasps all in a light embrace,
   And silently wanders away.

Come forth in the air divine,
   Thou dearest, my crown of bliss!
Give that flower-sweet cheek of thine
   To the morning breeze to kiss.

Add but thy perfect presence
   To gladden my happy eyes,
And I would not change earth's morning
   For the dawns of Paradise!

## IMPATIENCE

E. L.

ONLY to follow you, dearest, only to find you!
　　Only to feel for one instant the touch of your hand;
　Only to tell you once of the love you left behind
　　　you, —
　　　To say the world without you is like a desert of
　　　　sand;

That the flowers have lost their perfume, the rose its
　　　　splendor,
　　　And the charm of nature is lost in a dull eclipse;
　That joy went out with the glance of your eyes so
　　　　tender,
　　　And beauty passed with the lovely smile on your
　　　　lips.

I did not dream it was you who kindled the morning
　　　And folded the evening purple in peace so sweet;
　But you took the whole world's rapture without a
　　　　warning,
　　　And left me naught save the print of your patient
　　　　feet.

I count the days and the hours that hold us asunder:
　　　I long for Death's friendly hand which shall rend in
　　　　twain,

With the glorious lightning flash and the golden thun-
 der,
 These clouds of the earth, and give me my own
  again!


## IN THE LANE

By cottage walls the lilacs blow;
 Rich spikes of perfume stand and sway
 At open casements, where all day
The warm wind waves them to and fro.

Out of the shadow of the door,
 Into the golden morning air,
 Comes one who makes the day more fair
And summer sweeter than before.

The apple blossoms might have shed
 Upon her cheek the bloom so rare;
 The sun has kissed her bright brown hair
Braided about her graceful head.

Lightly betwixt the lilacs tall
 She passes, through the garden gate,
 Across the road, and stays to wait
A moment by the orchard wall;

And then in gracious light and shade,
  Beneath the blossom-laden trees,
  'Mid song of birds and hum of bees,
She strays, unconscious, unafraid,

Till swiftly o'er the grassy space
  Comes one whose step she fain would stay.
  Glad as the newly risen day
He stoops to read her drooping face.

Her face is like the morning skies,
  Bright, timid, tender, blushing sweet;
  She dares not trust her own to meet
The steady splendor of his eyes.

He holds her with resistless charm,
  With truth, with power, with beauty crowned;
  About her lovely shape is wound
The strong, safe girdle of his arm.

And up and down through shade and light
  They wander through the flying hours,
  And all the way is strewn with flowers,
And life looks like one long delight.

Ah, happy twain! No frost shall harm,
  No change shall reach your bliss, so long
  As keeps its place the faithful, strong,
Safe girdle of that folding arm.

Could you this simple secret know
  No death in life would be to fear,
  When you may watch, in some sad year,
By cottage walls the lilacs blow!


## HER MIRROR

O MIRROR, whence her lovely face
  Was wont to look with radiance sweet,
Hast thou not kept of her some trace,
  Some memory that thou mayest repeat?

Could I but find in thee once more
  Some token of her presence dear!
O mirror, wilt thou not restore
  Her shadow for an instant here?

Thou couldst not yield a boon so great.
  I see my own dim face and eyes
With love and longing desolate,
  All drowned in wistful memories.

Blindly for her dear hand I grope;
  There 's nothing life can have in store
So sweet to me as this sweet hope,
  To feel her smile on me once more!

# FOR CHRISTMAS

"THY own wish wish I thee in every place."
    The Christmas joy, the song, the feast, the cheer,
Thine be the light of love in every face
    That looks on thee, to bless thy coming year.

Thy own wish wish I thee.   What dost thou crave?
    All thy dear hopes be thine, whate'er they be.
A wish fulfilled may make thee king or slave;
    I wish thee Wisdom's eyes wherewith to see.

Behold, she stands and waits, the youthful year!
    A breeze of morning breathes about her brows;
She holds thy storm and sunshine, bliss and fear,
    Blossom and fruit upon the bending boughs.

She brings thee gifts.   What blessing wilt thou
        choose?
Life's crown of good in earth or heaven above,
The one immortal joy thou canst not lose,
    Is Love! Leave all the rest, and choose thou
        Love!

## AT SET OF MOON

THE wind blows from the stormy quarter and the
        moon is old.
Trouble has gathered in the sky so pallid, dim, and
        cold.
Can this be morning?   Is the world so blank and out
        of tune?
Down yonder dim horizon something fades beside the
        moon.

What is it?   'T is the ghost of joy that made the
        earth so sweet;
Life's one supreme, bright happiness, that hastes with
        flying feet.
The fading moon will brighten soon, in splendor shine
        again,
But joy that was the life of life is merged in bitter
        pain.

Last night I passed her window: she dreamed not I
        was near.
One ray slipped through the jealous curtain, rosy-warm
        and clear;
I kissed the flowers on which it fell, all dewy cold
        were they.
With patient anguish in my heart I turned and stole
        away.

She will not miss me, will not know if I am here or
    there;
If I am dead, or if I live, will neither know nor care.
Death is not bitter as my grief, which craves one sin-
    gle boon, —
Release me, God! let my life fade like yonder waning
    moon.


## MY GARDEN

It blossomed by the summer sea,
  A tiny space of tangled bloom
  Wherein so many flowers found room,
A miracle it seemed to be!

Up from the ground, alert and bright,
  The pansies laughed in gold and jet,
  Purple and pied, and mignonette
Breathed like a spirit of delight.

Flaming the rich nasturtiums ran
  Along the fence, and marigolds
  "Opened afresh their starry folds"
In beauty as the day began;

While ranks of scarlet poppies gay
  Waved when the soft south-wind did blow,

Superb in sunshine, to and fro,
Like soldiers proud in brave array.

And tall blue larkspur waved its spikes
Against the sea's deep violet,
That every breeze makes deeper yet
With splendid azure where it strikes;

And rosy-pale sweet-peas climbed up,
And phloxes spread their colors fine,
Pink, white, and purple, red as wine,
And fire burned in the eschscholtzia's cup.

More dear to me than words can tell
Was every cup and spray and leaf;
Too perfect for a life so brief
Seemed every star and bud and bell.

And many a maiden, fairer yet,
Came smiling to my garden gay,
Whose graceful head I decked alway
With pansy and with mignonette.

Such slender shapes of girlhood young
Haunted that little blooming space,
Each with a more delightful face
Than any flower that ever sprung!

O shadowy shapes of youthful bloom!
  How fair the sweet procession glides
  Down memory's swift and silent tides,
Till lost in doubtful mists of gloom!

Year after year new flowers unfold,
  Year after year fresh maidens fair,
  Scenting their perfume on the air,
Follow and find their red and gold.

And while for them the poppies' blaze
  I gather, brightening into mine
  The eyes of vanished beauty shine,
That gladdened long-lost summer days.

Where are they all who wide have ranged?
  Where are the flowers of other years?
  What ear the wistful question hears?
Ah, some are dead and all are changed.

And still the constant earth renews
  Her treasured splendor; still unfold
  Petals of purple and of gold
Beneath the sunshine and the dews.

But for her human children dear
  Whom she has folded to her breast,
  No beauty wakes them from their rest,
Nor change they with the changing year.

## LOST AND SAVED

"O Love," he whispered low, "Eternal Love!"
    And softly twilight's shadows round them drew,
And one by one the stars grew bright above,
    And warm airs from the gates of sunset blew.

Swift o'er the summer sea they lightly sailed;
    The rushing winds, the rushing waves, sang sweet;
But sweeter than all sounds the voice that failed,
    Shaken by the full heart that strongly beat.

Fast piled the clouds in darkness south and east,
    Each other's starry eyes they only saw.
What was the world to them?   The breeze increased,
    And caught the glimmering sail with gusty flaw.

Low stooped the mast; the firm hand at the helm
    Held bravely yet the light craft to its course,
Though hurrying breakers fain would overwhelm,
    And the gale gathered with resistless force.

Black night, black storm, that rose in sudden wrath!
    All lost the cheerful stars forgot to burn,
And death was waiting silent in the path,
    Along whose wavering way was no return.

Or life or death — what mattered it to them?
  Locked mute and still within each other's arms,
They sought no more the tempest's rage to stem,
  Deaf to the tumult of the night's alarms.

Beyond their fate uplifted, death was naught,
  Nor could they know, borne safe all pain above,
Into immortal life together caught,
  That only thus should live Eternal Love!

## A ROSE OF JOY

### FOR A BETROTHAL

As when one wears a fragrant rose
  Close to the heart, a rose most fair,
And while the day's life onward flows
  Forgets that it is fastened there,

And wonders what delicious charm
  Dwells in the air about, and whence
Come the rich wafts of perfume warm
  Subtly saluting soul and sense;

And then, remembering what it is,
  Bends smiling eyes the flower above,
Adores its beauty and its bliss
  And looks on it with grateful love —

Even so I wear, O friend of mine,
　The sweet thought of your happiness;
The knowledge of your joy divine
　Is fragrant with a power to bless.

With the day's work preoccupied
　Vaguely, half conscious of delight,
Upborne as on a buoyant tide,
　I wonder why life seems so bright.

Then memory speaks; then winter gray
　And age and cares that have no end
Touch me no more.　I am to-day
　Rich in the wealth that cheers my friend.


## IN SEPTEMBER

LEAPING from the boat, through the lazy, sparkling
　　surf,
Up the slope we press, o'er the rich, elastic turf.
Heavy waves the goldenrod in the morning breeze,
Swift spring the startled grasshoppers, thick about our
　　knees.

Look, how shines the distance!　Leagues of water
　　blue,
Wind-swept, sunshine-flooded, with a flying sail or
　　two,

Gleaming white as silver, and dreaming, here and
  there,
A snowy-breasted gull floats in the golden air.

How sweet to climb together the scented, flowery
  slope,
O dearest, hand in hand, like children following hope;
Laughing at the grasshoppers, singing with delight,
Only to be alive this September morning bright!

But where would be the beauty of this brilliant atmos-
  phere
Wert thou away, my darling?   Would not the sky be
  drear,
And gray the living azure of the changing, sparkling
  sea?
And blossoms, birds, and sails, and clouds — what
  would they be to me?

Rest we here a little upon the breezy height,
And watch the play of color, the shadow, and the
  light,
And let the lovely moment overflow us with its bliss.
When shall we find another so beautiful as this?

I turn from all the splendor to those clear eyes of
  thine,
That watch the shimmering sails on the far horizon
  line;

While sun and wind salute thy cheek till roses blos-
      som there,
Thou golden creature, than the morn a thousand times
      more fair!

Ah! must it end?   Must winter hurl its snow across
      the sea,
And roar with leagues of bitterness between thy face
      and me?
Must chill December fill with murk and storm this
      wooing air,
And the west-wind wail like the voice of some su-
      preme despair?

Too surely!   But, O friendly eyes, hold summer safe
      for me;
Only, O gentle heart, keep warm and sweet my mem-
      ory;
And no fury of the tempest my world can desolate —
This wingèd joy will lift my soul above the storms of
      fate.


## UNDER THE EAVES

PLEASANT above the city's din
   My quiet room beneath the eaves;
The first to see the day begin,
   The last the sunshine lingering leaves.

Pleasant upon the window pane
   Uplifted high, so near the sky,
To hear the patter of the rain,
   Or see the snow go swirling by;

To watch the gilded weathercocks
   In every eddy turn and wheel;
To hear the clear, melodious shocks
   Of chiming bells that clang and peal.

Dove-haunted roofs and towers and spires,
   The friendly faces of the clocks,
The network of electric wires,
   The sparrows gossiping in flocks,

The smoke's dim, ragged phantoms soft
   From myriad chimneys lightly curled,
That mingle with the clouds aloft
   Slow sailing with the sailing world —

Pleasant and peaceful all.   Most sweet
   When morning and when evening fires,
Silent above the busy street,
   Touch the dove-haunted roofs and spires.

Neighbored by sparrow and by dove,
   A comrade of the weathercocks,
My quiet, airy perch I love,
   The chimney-stacks, the city clocks;

And thank the heavens that bend above
  For leave to find such deep delight
In tower and spire and fluttering dove,
  Color and cloud and sparrow's flight.


## NOVEMBER MORNING

WITH clamor the wild southwester
  Through the wide heaven is roaring,
Ploughing the ocean, and over
  The earth its fury outpouring.

Lo, how the vast gray spaces
  Wrestle and roll and thunder,
Billow piled upon billow,
  Closing and tearing asunder,

As if the deep raged with the anger
  Of hosts of the fabulous kraken!
And the firm house shudders and trembles,
  Beaten, buffeted, shaken.

Battles the gull with the tempest,
  Struggling and wavering and faltering,
Soaring and striving and sinking,
  Turning, its high course altering.

Down through the cloudy heaven
  Notes from the wild geese are falling;
Cries like harsh bell-tones are ringing,
  Echoing, clanging, and calling.

Plunges the schooner landward,
  Swiftly the long seas crossing,
Close-reefed, seeking the harbor,
  Half lost in the spray she is tossing.

A rift in the roof of vapor!
  And stormy sunshine is streaming
To color the gray, wild water
  Like chrysoprase, green and gleaming.

Cold and tempestuous ocean,
  Ragged rock, brine-swept and lonely,
Grasp of the long, bitter winter —
  These things to gladden me only!

---

Love, dost thou wait for me in some rich land
  Where the gold orange hangs in odorous calm?
Where the clear waters kiss the flowery strand,
  Bordered with shining sand and groves of palm?

And while this bitter morning breaks for me,
  Draws to its close thy warm, delicious day;

Lights, colors, perfumes, music, joy, for thee,
    For me the cold, wild sea, the cloudy gray!

Rises the red moon in thy tranquil sky,
    Plashes the fountain with its silver talk,
And as the evening wind begins to sigh,
    Thy sweet girl's shape steals down the garden walk.

And through the scented dusk a white robe gleams,
    Lingering beneath the starry jasmine sprays,
Till where thy clustered roses breathe in dreams,
    A sudden gush of song thy light step stays.

That was the nightingale!   O Love of mine,
    Hear'st thou my voice in that pathetic song,
Throbbing in passionate cadences divine,
    Sinking to silence with its rapture strong?

I stretch my arms to thee through all the cold,
    Through all the dark, across the weary space
Between us, and thy slender form I fold,
    And gaze into the wonder of thy face.

Pure brow the moonbeam touches, tender eyes
    Splendid with feeling, delicate smiling mouth,
And heavy silken hair that darkly lies
    Soft as the twilight clouds in thy sweet South, —

O beautiful my Love!   In vain I seek
　To hold the heavenly dream that fades from me.
I needs must wake with salt spray on my cheek,
　Flung from the fury of this northern sea.


## IN DEATH'S DESPITE

WHITHER departs the perfume of the rose?
　Into what life dies music's golden sound?
Year after year life's long procession goes
　To hide itself beneath the senseless ground.
Upon the grave's inexorable brink
　Amazed with loss the human creature stands;
Vainly he strives to reason or to think,
　Left with his aching heart and empty hands;
He calls his lost in vain.   In sorrow drowned,
Darkness and silence all his sense confound.


Till in Death's roll-call stern he hears his name,
　In turn he follows and is lost to sight;
Though comforted by love and crowned by fame,
　He hears the summons dread no man may slight.
Sweetly and clear upon his quiet grave
　The birds shall sing, unmindful of his dust;
Softly in turn the long green grass shall wave
　Over his fallen head.   In turn he must
Submit to be forgotten, like the rest,
Though high the heart that beat within his breast.

The rose falls and the music's sound is gone;
   Dear voices cease, and clasp of loving hands;
Alone we stand when the brief day is done,
   Searching with saddened eyes earth's darkening
      lands.
Worthless as is the lightest fallen leaf
   We seem, yet constant as the night's first star
Kindles our deathless hope, and from our grief
   Is born the trust no misery can mar,
That Love shall lift us all despair above,
Shall conquer death, — yea, Love, and only Love!


## A SONG OF HOPE

THE morning breaks, the storm is past.   Behold!
   Along the west the lift grows bright, — the sea
Leaps sparkling blue to catch the sunshine's gold,
   And swift before the breeze the vapors flee.

Light cloud-flocks white that troop in joyful haste
   Up and across the pure and tender sky;
Light laughing waves that dimple all the waste
   And break upon the rocks and hurry by!

Flying of sails, of clouds, a tumult sweet,
   Wet, tossing buoys, a warm wild wind that blows

The pennon out and rushes on to greet
　Thy lovely cheek and heighten its soft rose!

Beloved, beloved! Is there no morning breeze
　To clear our sky and chase our mists away,
Like this great air that sweeps the freshening seas,
　And wakes the old sad world to glad new day?

Sweeter than morning, stronger than the gale,
　Deeper than ocean, warmer than the sun,
My love shall climb, shall claim thee, shall prevail
　Against eternal darkness, dearest one!

## OUR SOLDIERS

PEACE smiles over hamlet and city,
　Peace broods over mountain and stream,
Our tears of anguish and pity
　Are a half-forgotten dream.
The tempest of battle is ended,
　And our dear, delivered land
Stands free in the sunshine splendid,
　No stain upon her hand.

What shall we do to honor
　Her dauntless sons to-day,
Who shed such glory upon her,
　Striking her chains away?

Fair floats the banner o'er her, —
　　What did not her children give?
They cast their lives before her,
　　Dying that she might live.

Remember them, praise them, love them,
　　The noble hearts and brave!
May earth lie lightly above them
　　In many a nameless grave.
Great was their high endeavor,
　　Great is their glorious meed;
Honor our heroes forever,
　　Praise them with word and deed!


## TWO

SHE turned the letter's rustling page; her smile
　　Made bright the air about her while she read:
"I come to you to-morrow, love; meanwhile
　　Love me, my sweet," he said.

"What other business has my life?" she thought,
　　And musing passed, as in some happy dream,
To the day's care and toils, and while she wrought
　　Time winged with light did seem.

To-morrow!　When the summer morning broke
　　In rose and gold, and touched her slumbering eyes

Softly, with tempered splendor, and she woke
    To the rich dawn's surprise,

Birds sang aloft and roses bloomed below;
    Flushed wide the tender fleecy mists above;
Came Memory, leading Hope, and whispered low,
    "Love me!   I come, my love."

"So that thou comest," she thought, "skies may grow
       gray,
    The sun may fade, the sea with foam blanch white,
Tempest and thunder dread may spoil the day,
    But not my deep delight."

O sweet and awful Love!   O power supreme,
    Mighty and sacred, terrible art thou!
Beside thee Life and Death are but a dream;
    Before thee all must bow.

When in the west the sunset's crimson flame
    Burned low and wasted, and the cool winds blew,
Watching the steadfast sky she heard her name
    Breathed in the voice she knew.

Joy shook her heart, nor would its pulse be stilled;
    Her fair cheek borrowed swift the sunset's bloom.
A presence beautiful and stately filled
    The silence of the room.

"Hast thou no word of welcome?" for indeed
  Like some mute marble goddess proud stood she;
She turned. "O king of men!" she cried, "what
     need
  That I should welcome thee?"

Her eyes divine beneath her solemn brows
  Met his clear gaze and measured strength for
     strength.
She drooped, as to the sun the lily bows,
  Into his arms at length.

Wide swung heaven's gates for them; no more they
     knew.
  The silent stars looked in, they saw them not.
The slow winds wandered soft through dusk and dew,
  But earth was all forgot.


## COMPENSATION

In that new world toward which our feet are set,
Shall we find aught to make our hearts forget
Earth's homely joys and her bright hours of bliss?
Has heaven a spell divine enough for this?
For who the pleasure of the spring shall tell,
When on the leafless stalk the brown buds swell,
When the grass brightens and the days grow long,
And little birds break out in rippling song?

Oh sweet the dropping eve, the blush of morn,
The starlit sky, the rustling fields of corn,
The soft airs blowing from the freshening seas,
The sun-flecked shadow of the stately trees,
The mellow thunder and the lulling rain,
The warm, delicious, happy summer rain,
When the grass brightens and the days grow long,
And little birds break out in rippling song!

O beauty manifold, from morn till night,
Dawn's flush, noon's blaze, and sunset's tender light!
O fair, familiar features, changes sweet
Of her revolving seasons, storm and sleet
And golden calm, as slow she wheels through space
From snow to roses, — and how dear her face
When the grass brightens and the days grow long,
And little birds break out in rippling song!

O happy Earth!   O home so well beloved!
What recompense have we, from thee removed?
One hope we have that overtops the whole, —
The hope of finding every vanished soul
We love and long for daily, and for this
Gladly we turn from thee and all thy bliss,
Even at thy loveliest, when the days are long,
And little birds break out in rippling song.

## SONNET

BACK from life's coasts the ebbing tide had drawn,
  The singing tide that brimmed with joy the shore:
The torch of sunset and the blush of dawn
  Seemed to have lost their glow forevermore,
There was such silence in the empty sky!
  And Nature mocked me, grown so cold and dumb,
And Faith, I thought, had perished utterly,
  Nor knew I whence a ray of hope should come;
When, like a royal messenger of good
  Sent to some sad and famine-stricken land,
Across my threshold dark you passed, and stood,
  Bearing the keys of heaven in your hand;
And wide the bright, resounding gates you threw!
Tell me, O friend, what I shall do for you!


## JOY

Joy breathes in the sweet airs of spring,
  And in the shy wild blossom hides,
And soars upon the swallow's wing,
  And with the singing water glides.

Where lilies stand, a fragrant crowd,
  Rocked by the warm south wind he lies;

And dreams upon the balmy cloud
  Soft floating in the tender skies;

Shines clear from out the crescent sharp,
  Glittering above the sunset's red,
And of the west wind makes a harp,
  And gleams in starlight overhead.

Joy mantles in the golden wine,
  Joy to earth's humblest doth descend,
And looks at me with cheer divine
  From out the dear eyes of my friend.


## BELOVED

A strong sweet tide toward the lonely shore
  Sets steadfastly, till every inlet sings,
And to the waiting silence, blank before,
    Its full refreshment brings.

Through the day's business passing to and fro,
  Ever she grows more conscious of the charm
Upholding her wherever she may go,
    Like some enfolding arm.

For this dear joy all days more fair do seem,
  The night's repose more blissful and more deep,

As pillowed on the breast of this sweet dream
      Softly she falls asleep.

Safe is she, lifted all earth's ills above;
  No storm can break her calm, no evil reach
Within the charmèd circle drawn by Love,
      Blest beyond thought or speech.

O maiden, dream thy dream!   Life's crown of thorns,
  Draws it not down, unseen, about thy brows?
The glory of thy summer eves and morns
      Stern winter shall espouse.

Within this Eden of thy sweet content
  No mortal stays, — that, the great gods forbid;
But canst thou learn that in thy banishment
      A higher good lies hid?

## THE ANSWER

    THE blossoms blush on the bough,
      And the air is full of song,
  Oh give me my answer now,
      Dear Love, I have waited long!

  The blossoms mantle and flush, —
      I see but the rose in your cheek, —

And the birds their music hush,
　For the fate your lips may speak.

I listen for life or death,
　With hope's deep rapture stirred,
And faint as the blossoms' breath
　Comes your low, delicious word.

And the earth reels under my feet, —
　O blossoms that burn on the bough! —
With the strength of a joy so sweet,
　For I have my answer now!


## SONG

PAST the point and by the beach,
　Oh but the waves ran merrily,
With laughter light and silver speech,
　And red the sunset flushed the sea.

Two lovers wandered side by side, —
　Oh but the waves ran merrily;
They watched the rushing of the tide,
　And fairer than a dream was she.

About her slender waist was cast —
　Oh but the waves ran merrily —

His strong right arm that held her fast,
  A zone that clasped her royally.


He gazed in her bewildering face,—
  Oh but the waves ran merrily:
"See how the waves each other chase!
  So follow all my thoughts to thee."


"And seest thou yonder star?" she said,—
  Oh but the waves ran merrily,—
"Superb in yonder evening-red?
  So dost thou light my life for me!"


'T was long ago that star did shine,—
  Oh but the waves ran merrily;
Love made for them the world divine
  In that old time beside the sea.


The soft wind sighs, the great sea rolls,—
  Oh but the waves run merrily;
What has Time done with those two souls?
  And Love, who charmed them, where is he?


## AUGUST

BUTTERCUP nodded and said good-by,
  Clover and daisy went off together,
But the fragrant water-lilies lie
  Yet moored in the golden August weather.

The swallows chatter about their flight,
  The cricket chirps like a rare good fellow,
The asters twinkle in clusters bright,
  While the corn grows ripe and the apples mellow.


## SONG

A BIRD upon a rosy bough
  Sang low and long, sang late and loud,
Until the young moon's silver prow
  Was lost behind a bar of cloud.

The south wind paused and held its breath —
  Sing loud and late, sing low and long —
While sweet as Love and sad as Death
  The matchless notes rose wild and strong.

They rang with rapture, loss and change, —
  Sing low and late, sing long and loud —
A tumult passionate and strange,
  A speechless grief, a patience proud;

Till with "farewell for evermore," —
  Sing late and loud, sing low and long, —
Like waves that kiss a barren shore
  In sobbing cadence died the song.

## "OH TELL ME NOT OF HEAVENLY HALLS"

OH tell me not of heavenly halls,
  Of streets of pearl and gates of gold,
Where angel unto angel calls
  'Mid splendors of the sky untold;

My homesick heart would backward turn
  To find this dear, familiar earth,
To watch its sacred hearth-fires burn,
  To catch its songs of joy or mirth.

I 'd lean from out the heavenly choir
  To hear once more the red cock crow,
What time the morning's rosy fire
  O'er hill and field began to glow.

To hear the ripple of the rain,
  The summer waves at ocean's brim,
To hear the sparrow sing again
  I 'd quit the wide-eyed cherubim!

I care not what heaven's glories are;
  Content am I.   More joy it brings
To watch the dandelion's star
  Than mystic Saturn's golden rings.

And yet — and yet, O dearest one!
   My comfort from life's earliest breath —
To follow thee where thou art gone
   Through those dim, awful gates of Death,

To find thee, feel thy smile again,
   To have eternity's long day
To tell my grateful love, — why, then,
   Both heaven and earth might pass away!


## MIDSUMMER

WHITE as a blossom is the kerchief quaint
   Over her sumptuous shoulders lightly laid;
Fairer than any picture men could paint,
   In the cool orchard's fragrant light and shade

She stands and waits: some pensive dream enfolds
   Her beauty sweet, and bows her radiant head;
The delicate pale roses that she holds
   Seem to have borrowed of her cheek their red.

She waits like some superb but drooping flower
   To feel the touch of morning and the sun,
And o'er her head the glowing petals shower,
   And to her feet the shifting sunbeams run.

I follow to her feet their pathway fine,
    And while my voice the charmèd silence breaks,
What startled splendors from her deep eyes shine!
    Into what glory my rich flower awakes!


## NEW YEAR SONG

O Sorrow, go thy way and leave me!
    Weary am I of thee, thou Sorrow old.
Unclasp thy hand from mine and cease to grieve me,
    Fade like the winter sunset dim and cold.

Depart, and trouble me no longer!
    Die! Vanish with forgotten yesterdays.
Eastward the darkness melts, the light grows stronger,
    And dawn breaks sweet across the shrouding haze.

Die and depart, Old Year, old Sorrow!
    Welcome, O morning air of health and strength!
O glad New Year, bring us new hope to-morrow,
    With blossom, leaf, and fruitage bright at length.


## CAPTURED

Nanette!
Can you not teach me to forget?
It is so hard to understand!
You would not lift your slender hand

To keep me yours, yet must I be
Yours only, yours eternally,
Though 'neath the chain I strive and fret,
Nanette!
That golden hour when first we met,
Like the swift inundating sea
Love's tide swept in and conquered me.
Love uttered Love's supremest word,
A moment you were touched and stirred;
Ah, that 's the anguish of regret,
Nanette!
My every thought on you was set;
I poured for you Love's priceless wine,
You could no more its power divine
Than one small blossom's cup of gold
The boundless firmament could hold:
My eyes with scornful tears are wet,
Nanette!
This withered spray of mignonette
You gave me, from my heart I take,
This sick, sad heart you taught to ache,
And fling it in the restless sea —
I would my thought of you could be
So flung away from me; and yet,
Nanette!
I cannot break the cruel net,
Though I may curse my fate and swear
You are not kind, nor good, nor fair,

You 'll hold me by one silken tress,
Or eyelid's down-dropped loveliness,
A touch of hand, or tone of voice,
Or smile that all my will destroys:
Ah Heaven! the only boon I crave
Is rest, the silence of the grave.
Release me!   Teach me to forget,
Nanette!


# FAITH

FAIN would I hold my lamp of life aloft
  Like yonder tower built high above the reef;
Steadfast, though tempests rave or winds blow soft,
  Clear, though the sky dissolve in tears of grief.

For darkness passes, storms shall not abide:
  A little patience and the fog is past.
After the sorrow of the ebbing tide
  The singing flood returns in joy at last.

The night is long and pain weighs heavily,
  But God will hold his world above despair.
Look to the East, where up the lucid sky
  The morning climbs!   The day shall yet be fair!

## AT DAWN

EARLY this morning waking,
  I heard the sandpipers call,
And the sea on the shore was breaking
  With a dreamy rise and fall.

The dawn that was softly blushing
  Touched cloud and wave with rose,
And the sails in the west were flushing,
  No breeze stirred their repose.

What tone in the water's falling
  Had reached me while I dreamed?
What sound in the wild birds' calling
  Like a heavenly greeting seemed?

What meant the delicate splendor
  That brightened the conscious morn
With a radiance fresh and tender
  Crowning the day newborn?

All nature's musical voices
  Whispered, "Awake and see!
Awake, for the day rejoices!"
  What news had the morn for me?

Then I remembered the blessing
So sweet, O friend, so near!
The joy beyond all expressing, —
To-day you would be here.


## IN A HORSE-CAR

I WONDERED what power possessed the place
    As I took my seat in the motley crowd,
And glancing swiftly from face to face
    Of the poor and mean, and the rich and proud,

And all the stages betwixt the two
    That daily travel the iron track,
I stopped at a young face fresh as dew,
    Framed in white with a hood of black.

'T was a little Sister of Charity;
    Oh young and slender, oh sweet and calm!
Like a pensive moonbeam pale was she,
    With her fair hands folded palm to palm.

And a delicate beauty of high repose,
    A sacred peace, as if far withdrawn
From the hard world's din, like a cloistered rose,
    She blossomed pure as the breath of dawn.

I marveled much how a girl like this
  In her Maytime splendor could turn away
From the brimming cup of her youth's bright bliss,
  To succor the sorrowful day by day.

And yet when I looked at her once more,
  With her lofty aspect of tempered cheer,
All the joys of the earth seemed vain and poor
  To the lovely record written here.

And I felt how true it is, how sure
  That every good deed adds a light
To the human face, not there before,
  While every ill thing leaves its blight.

It does not follow that women and men
  Must live in a cloister to work for God;
There 's enough to do, to the dullest ken,
  In the great world's paths spread wide abroad.

And the good or ill of the life we lead
  Is sculptured clear on the countenance;
Be it love and goodness, or sin and greed,
  Who runs may read at a single glance.

## A VALENTINE

WHAT is the whole world worth, Dear,
    Weighed against love and truth?
Sweet is the spring to the earth, Dear,
    Bright is the blossom of youth:

And the skies of summer are tender
    In fullness of life and strength,
And rich is the autumn splendor,
    But winter comes at length.

Tell me, what spell shall charm us
    When the golden days expire?
What is there left to warm us
    Save Love's most sacred fire?

While on the soul's high altar
    Its clear light burns secure,
Though the step of joy may falter,
    And the glad years are no more,

The frosts of age are naught, Dear!
    I clasp thy hand in mine
Fondly as when youth sought, Dear,
    To be thy Valentine.

## WITHIN AND WITHOUT

THE tide flows up, the tide flows down:
The water brims the creek and falls;
A cottage weather-stained and brown
Lifts at the brink its time-worn walls.

Beneath the lowly window sill
Two little beds of blossoms gay
The wandering airs with fragrance fill,
Sweeten the night and charm the day.

The tide flows up, the tide flows down:
From the low window's humble square
A woman in a faded gown,
With care-dimmed eyes and tangled hair,

Looks out across the smiling space
Where golden suns and stars unfold:
Blue larkspur, the pied pansy's face,
Nasturtium bells of scarlet bold, —

She sees them not, nor cares, nor knows.
A man's rough figure noon and night
And morning o'er the threshold goes, —
No sense has he for their delight.

The tide flows up, the tide flows down:
In that dull house a little maid
Lives lonely, under Fortune's frown,
A life unchildlike and afraid.

To her that tiny garden-plot
Means heaven.   She comes at eve to stand
'Mid mallow and forget-me-not
And marigolds on either hand.

They look at her with brilliant eyes,
Their scent is greeting and caress;
They spread their rich and glowing dyes
Her saddened soul to cheer and bless.

The tide flows up, the tide flows down:
Within, how base the life and poor!
Without, what wealth and beauty crown
The humble flowers beside the door!


## BETROTHED

SOFTLY the flickering firelight comes and goes;
  The warm glow flashes, sinks, departs, returns,
And shows me where the delicate red rose
  In the tall, slender vase of crystal burns.

The tempest beats without.    The hush within
   Is sweeter for the turmoil of the night;
Ice clatters at the pane and snowflakes spin
   A web of woven storm, a shroud of white.

Its secret the wild winter weather keeps,
   No sound transpires except the tempest's breath;
Locked in the frost the muffled pathway sleeps,
   For any human token still as death.

My eyes the room's familiar aspect hold,
   Its quiet beauty and its sumptuous gloom,
Its glimmering draperies of dull rich gold,
   The gleam upon the burnished peacock's plume.

My rose, my book, my work, I see them all,
   With my whole soul surrendered to one sense,
My life within my ears, for one footfall
   Listening with patience breathless and intense.

'T is my heart hears, at last, the silent door
   Swing on its hinges, there 's no need the fire
Should show me whose step thrills the conscious floor,
   As suddenly the wayward flame leaps higher.

Thou comest, bringing all good things that are!
   Infinite joy, and peace with white wings furled,
All heaven is here and thou the morning-star,
   Thou splendor of my life! "Thou Day o' the world!"

## QUESTIONS

THE steadfast planet spins through space,
　　And into darkness, into light
Swiftly it wheels its living face:
　　" 'T is day," we say, or "It is night."

And we who cling and with it turn,
　　Till spent is our brief span of years,
Watching our sister stars that burn
　　Through the dim trouble of our tears,

We question of the silence vast,
　　Of souls that people distant spheres;
What of their future and their past?
　　Have they our sorrows, joys, and fears?

Do the same flowers make glad their sight?
　　The same birds sing?　On their great seas
Do ships like ours, with canvas white,
　　Move stately, answering to the breeze?

Have they their Christ, their Christmas Day?
　　Know they Mahomet?　Buddha?　One,
Or all or none?　And do they pray?
　　And have they wrought as we have done?

We cannot guess; 't is hard indeed,
  Our own orb's tale of its dim past
Through centuries untold to read,
  And who its future shall forecast?

We only know it keeps its place,
  An atom in the universe,
As through the awful realms of space
  The mighty hosts of stars disperse.

We know the hand that holds in check
  The whirling worlds, each in its course,
And saves the universe from wreck
  And peril, this tremendous Force

Holds likewise all our little lives;
  The suns and stars do all obey
His bidding, never planet strives
  To swerve from its appointed way.

The dangerous boon alone to us
  Is given, to choose 'twixt ill and well,
Rebellion or obedience, — thus
  To build our heaven, or dig our hell.

But one great thought our strength upholds:
  Nothing shall perish!  Though his rod
Smites sore, his mercy still enfolds
  His own; God's souls are safe with God.

## TYRE AND SIDON

BE thou ashamed, O Sidon, saith the sea!
    The loud voice of the world is in thine ears,
The world thy service hath and ruleth thee,
    Thou givest unto vanity thy years.

Hearken, O Tyre!   For God stretched forth his hand
    Over the sea and He the kingdoms shook,
The broad earth quaked at breath of his command,
    From thy proud head the gleaming crown He took.

Is this the joyous city wont to boast
    Antiquity of ancient days?   Behold
Her feet shall carry her afar, her ghost
    Shall mourn in desolation and in cold.

Because the promise of Eternal life
    And endless glory and unchanging good
Was naught to her, and she chose sin and strife,
    Vain mocking shows, and empty husks for food;

Because so eagerly she served the world
    Choosing the base and temporal things it gave,
Down from her throne her haughtiness is hurled,
    And all her pride is leveled to a grave.

## HJELMA

STANDS Hjelma at her lady's chair,
    Serving with ready hands,
About her head her shining hair
    Braided in golden strands.

A rose blooms in her maiden cheek,
    And on her mouth's repose
A sweet content she cannot speak
    Is lovelier than the rose.

"What is that shrill and sudden cry,
    My little maiden? Say!"
"The wild wind shakes the windows high,
    And tears the sea to spray;

"Oh see you not the black, black sky,
    My mistress dear?" cries she.
"The squall comes down, the waves run high;
    Oh hear you not the sea?

"Oh glad am I the boats are in,
    And little Nils and Lars
Are safe, before the waves begin
    To leap across the stars!"

And up and down and here and there
  She goes with willing feet,
So busy, with that gentle air
  Of still contentment sweet!

At the far reef, since morning light,
  All day her brothers twain
About the wreck of yesternight
  Have worked with might and main.

She knows not when the cruel gale
  Made wild the waning day,
It seized upon their shivering sail
  And flung their skiff away.

She knows not they are driven, lost,
  Over the roaring brine,
Toward the dim, billow-beaten coast,
  While heaven will make no sign,

But scatters down its freezing snow
  To hide the fading light,
And drives its hurricane below
  To fright the shuddering night.

She hums her sweet Norwegian songs,
  She lights the lamps, and smiles;

The breakers rush in raging throngs
   Across the lonely miles.

And where is handsome Lars, so tall?
   And where is Nils, so dear?
Upon her soul no shadows fall,
   Nor any hint of fear.

And who shall speak to break the spell?
   And who will deal the blow?
The brothers twain she loved so well,
   Their fate must Hjelma know!

Loud thunders on the savage storm,
   With deep, defiant roar;
Unconscious in her shelter warm
   She hears it lash the shore.

And brightly shines her braided hair,
   And on her mouth's repose
Is sweet content, untouched by care,
   And on her cheek the rose.

## MY HOLLYHOCK

Ah me, my scarlet hollyhock,
Whose stately head the breezes rock,
How sad, that in one night of frost

Thy radiant beauty shall be lost,
And all thy glory overthrown
Ere half thy ruby buds have blown!
All day across my window low
Thy flowery stalk sways to and fro
Against a background of blue sea.
On the south wind, to visit thee,
Come airy shapes in sumptuous dyes, —
Rich golden, black-edged butterflies,
And humming-birds in emerald coats,
With flecks of fire upon their throats,
That in the sunshine whir and glance,
And probe the flowers with slender lance;
And many a drunken, drowsy bee,
Singing his song hilariously.
About the garden fluttering yet,
In amber plumage freaked with jet,
The goldfinches charm all the air
With sweet, sad crying everywhere.
To the dry sunflower stalks they cling,
And on the ripened disks they swing;
With delicate delight they feed
On the rich store of milky seed.

Autumn goes loitering through the land,
A torch of fire within her hand.
Soft sleeps the bloomy haze that broods
O'er distant hills and mellowing woods;

Rustle the cornfields far and near,
And nuts are ripe, and pastures sere,
And lovely odors haunt the breeze,
Borne o'er the sea and through the trees.
Belated beauty, lingering still
So near the edge of winter's chill,
The deadly daggers of the cold
Approach thee, and the year grows old.
Is it because I love thee so
Thou waitest, waving to and fro
Thy flowery spike, to gladden me,
Against the background of blue sea?
I wonder — hast thou not some sense,
Some measure of intelligence
Responding to my joy in thee?
Almost I dream that it may be,
Such subtleties are Nature's, hid
Her most well-trodden paths amid;
Such sympathies along her nerves;
Such sweetness in her fine reserves.
Howe'er it be, I thank the powers
That gave me such enchanted hours
This late October, watching thee
Wave thy bright flowers against the sea.

## BENEDICTION

"Oh heaven bless you, heaven keep you, sweet!"
    It was God's hand that dropped the healing balm
Upon her head, and clothed in prayerful calm
    Her soul as saints are robed from head to feet.

Gone is the beautiful beloved voice
    That spake that blessing in the vanished years;
Yet in her grateful memory still she hears
    The tender tones that made her heart rejoice.

And ever will, while memory keeps her seat;
    And though she dwelt among the nameless dead,
Her dust would thrill beneath the voice that said,
    "May heaven bless you, heaven keep you, sweet!"

## SONNET

If I do speak your praise, forgive me, Sweet!
    Since love demands expression, let me say
How joyfully my heart goes out to greet
    Your grace and charm with every changing day:
How sweet your morning kiss, how dear your smile,
    And tender touch, and voice that's low and clear,

And with what deep content I yield the while
    You draw me to you, near and yet more near,
And show me what pure depths within you lie, —
    The powers of good, the gentle steadfastness,
The quiet wisdom and the purpose high,
    So strong to love, to lift, to cheer and bless;
While like a robe of loveliness you wear
Your flower-like radiance delicately fair.


## ON THE TRAIN

THROUGH the storm, through the wind and the rain
Rushes the clattering train;
Past the hills, across valley and plain,
Through city and hamlet again,
With a rumble and roar we speed on
Till the half of our journey is done.

Close wrapped in my corner I dream,
Watching the raindrops stream
O'er the misty pane, and the gleam
Of the white of the steam,
As they hurry past and are lost,
On the wings of the tempest tossed.

Through the smoke and the din and the blur
Fast, fast I am flying to her!

All the thunder, the rattle and whir,
The noisy discomfort, the stir,
Are nothing to me, for my sense
Is lost in a rapture intense.

And like golden bees through the storm
Sweet memories cluster and swarm;
Sweet thoughts round a maidenly form
That I see by the firelight warm, —
Bright eyes that are watching the clock,
Little ears that are waiting my knock;

And I know how the color will rush
In that beautiful mantling blush
To her cheek, till its delicate flush
Shall rival the rose, as I hush
With a word her heart's tumult divine
And she lays her white hand within mine

Then thunder, thou clattering train,
And roar through the wind and the rain,
Past the hills, across valley and plain
Devour the long leagues! — till again
In the light of my love's happy eyes
The sun of my life shall arise.

## PEACE

Calm of the autumn night,
  With the glow of a primrose sky
Drowned in a sea of golden light
  From the harvest moon on high!

Against the rose of the sky
  Winging their silent way,
Darkly the gulls go floating by
  In the glow of the dying day.

Infinite peace and calm
  In the breast of the ocean wide,
In the air like delicate balm,
  In the faint, sweep lapse of the tide.

With the cricket's pensive sound,
  With the breath of the late, last rose,
Comes a sense of joy profound,
  And a bliss of deep repose.

What is thy mystic charm,
  O beautiful autumn night!
Not the sigh of the south wind warm,
  Not thy harvest moon's pure light;

Not the calm of the glassy sea,
   Reflecting thy stars above;
Nor thy perfumes borne to me
   On the balmy air I love:

But the soul of all thou art
   Calls to the soul in me,
And speaks to my quiet heart
   With the voice of sky and sea.


## AS LINNETS SING

NAY, wherefore should I seek thy patient ear
   To weary thee with words that naught avail!
This faltering voice will not ring true and clear,
   It will but break and fail.

And yet I cannot keep back any part
   Of my delight; fain would I give thee all
The music that thou makest in my heart,
   As David sang to Saul.

Would bring thee garlands sweet and manifold,
   Meek violets full of fragrance, — roses, too,
Dark pansies richly streaked with burning gold,
   And lilies bright with dew.

But ah, they grow so pallid 'neath my hand!
    So scentless and so colorless and frail —
The music cannot reach where thou dost stand,
        It will but break and fail.


Still at their source the notes are true and strong,
    And as some linnet sings, whose happy breast,
Filled with the summer's rapture, thrills with song
        That will not be suppressed,


Until she cannot choose but strive to blend
    Her slender silver thread of wavering sound
With all the nobler voices that ascend,
        Though lost it be and drowned, —


So sing I to the sun that fills my sky
    With warmth and light and health.    So I to thee
Send up my broken music ceaselessly,
        Silent I cannot be.


## RUTH


A BABY girl not two years old
    Among the phlox and pansies stands,
And full of flowers as they can hold
    Her mother fills her little hands,


And bids her cross to where I stay
    Within my garden's fragrant space,

And guides her past the poppies gay
  'Mid mazes of the blooming place,

Saying, " Go carry Thea these ! "
  Delighted, forth the baby fares,
Between the fluttering-winged sweet peas
  Her treasured buds she safely bears.

'T is but a step, but oh, what stress
  Of care !   What difficulties wait !
How many pretty dangers press
  Upon the path from gate to gate !

But high above her sunny head
  She tries the roses sweet to hold,
Now caught in coreopsis red,
  Half wrecked upon a marigold,

Or tangled in a cornflower tall,
  Or hindered by the poppy-tops, —
She struggles on, nor does she fall,
  Nor stalk nor stem her progress stops,

Until at last, the trials past,
  Victorious o'er the path's alarms,
Herself, her flowers and all are cast
  Breathless into my happy arms.

My smiling, rosy little maid !
And while her joy-flushed cheek I kiss,
And close to mine its bloom is laid,
I think, " So may you find your bliss,

" My precious !   When in coming years
Life's path grows a bewildering maze,
So may you conquer doubts and fears
And safely thread its devious ways,

" And find yourself, all dangers past,
Clasped to a fonder breast than mine,
And gain your heavenly joy at last
Safe in the arms of Love Divine."

## PETITION

My little grandson three years old
Sleeps by my bedside nightly,
Through the long hours of dark and cold,
Dreaming he slumbers lightly.

He feels my love around him fold,
And in its heart reposes,
Upon his hair a gleam of gold,
His cheeks like damask roses.

All through the chill and silent night
  I stretch a hand caressing,
To draw the blanket, warm and light,
  About him, with a blessing.

In sleep he knows that touch so sweet,
  So lingering and tender,
Turns his dear face my palm to meet,
  With soft and glad surrender.

O God of pity and of love,
  Have patience with our blindness,
Thy hand is stretched our heads above
  Warm with Thy watchful kindness.

Give us this baby's perfect faith!
  Whatever ills assail us,
Help us to feel, in life or death,
  That Thou wilt never fail us.


## APPEAL

THE childish voice rose to my ear
  Sweet toned and eager, praying me,
"I am so little, Granna dear,
  Please lift me up, so I can see."

I looked down at the pleading face,
   Felt the small hand's entreating touch,
And stooping caught in swift embrace
   The baby boy I loved so much,

And held him high that he might gaze
   At the great pageant of the sky,
The glory of the sunset's blaze,
   The glittering moon that curved on high.

With speechless love I clasped him close
   And read their beauty in his eyes,
And on his fair cheek kissed the rose,
   Sweeter than blooms of Paradise.

And in my heart his eager prayer
   Found echo, and the self-same cry
Rose from my heart through heaven's air,
   " O gracious Father, lift me high !

" So little and so low am I,
   Among earth's mists I call to Thee,
Show me the glory of Thy sky !
   Oh lift me up that I may see ! "

# INDEX OF TITLES

# INDEX OF FIRST LINES

# FROM
## *THE HEAVENLY GUEST*

# THE HEAVENLY GUEST

THE winter night shuts swiftly down. Within his little humble
   room
Martin, the good old shoemaker, sits musing in the gathering
   gloom.
His tiny lamp from off its hook he takes, and lights its friendly
   beam,
Reaches for his beloved book and reads it by the flickering gleam.

Long pores he o'er the sacred page. At last he lifts his shaggy head.
"If unto me the Master came, how should l welcome Him?" he said;
"Should I be like the Pharisee, with selfish thoughts filled to the
   brim,
Or like the sorrowing sinner,—she who weeping ministered to
   Him?"

He laid his head upon his arms, and while he thought, upon him
   crept
Slumber so gentle and so soft he did not realize he slept
"Martin!" he heard a low voice call. He started, looked toward the
   door:
No one was there. He dozed again. "Martin!" he heard it call once
   more.

"Martin, to-morrow I will come. Look out upon the street for me."
He rose, and slowly rubbed his eyes, and gazed about him drowsily.
"I dreamed," he said, and went to rest. Waking betimes with
   morning light,
He wondered, "Were they but a dream, the words I seemed to hear
   last night?"

Then, working by his window low, he watched the passers to and
   fro.
Poor Stephen, feeble, bent and old, was shoveling away the snow;

Martin at last laughed at himself for watching all so eagerly.
"What fool am I! What look I for? Think I the Master's face to see?

"I must be going daft, indeed!" He turned him to his work once
   more,
And stitched awhile, but presently found he was watching as before.
Old Stephen leaned against the wall; weary and out of breath was
   he.
"Come in, friend," Martin cried, "come, rest, and warm yourself,
   and have some tea."

"May Christ reward you!" Stephen said, rejoicing in the welcome
   heat;
"I was so tired!" "Sit," Martin begged, "be comforted and drink and
   eat."
But even while his grateful guest refreshed his chilled and toil-worn
   frame
Did Martin's eyes still strive to scan each passing form that went and
   came.

"Are you expecting somebody?" old Stephen asked. And Martin
   told,
Though half ashamed, his last night's dream. "Truly, I am not quite
   so bold
As to expect a thing like that," he said, "yet, somehow, still I look!"
With that from off its shelf he took his worn and precious Holy
   Book.

"Yesterday I was reading here, how among simple folk He walked
Of old, and taught them. Do you know about it? No?" So then he
   talked
With joy to Stephen. "Jesus said, 'The kind, the generous, the poor,
Blessed are they, the humble souls, to be exalted ever more.'"

With tears of gladness in his eyes poor Stephen rose and went his
   way,

His soul and body comforted; and quietly passed on the day,
Till Martin from his window saw a woman shivering in the cold,
Trying to shield her little babe with her thin garment worn and old.

He called her in and fed her, too, and while she ate he did his best
To make the tiny baby smile, that she might have a little rest;
"Now may Christ bless you, sir!" she cried, when warmed and
    cheered she would have gone;
He took his old cloak from the wall. "'Twill keep the cold out.
Put it on."

She wept. "Christ led you to look out and pity wretched me," said
    she.
Martin replied, "Indeed He did!" and told his story earnestly,
How the low voice said, "I will come," and he had watched the live-
    long day.
"All things are possible," she said, and then she, also, went her way.

Once more he sat him down to work, and on the passers-by to look,
Till the night fell, and then again he lit his lamp and took his book.
Another happy hour was spent, when all at once he seemed to hear
A rustling sound behind his chair; he listened, without thought of
    fear.

He peered about. Did something move in yonder corner dim and
    dark?
Was that a voice that spoke his name? "Did you not know me,
    Martin?" "Hark!
Who spoke?" cried Martin. "It is I," replied the Voice, and Stephen
    stepped
Forth from the dusk and smiled at him, and Martin's heart within
    him leapt!

Then like a cloud was Stephen gone, and once again did Martin
    hear

That heavenly Voice. "And this is I," sounded in tones divinely clear.
From out the darkness softly came the woman with the little child,
Gazing at him with gentle eyes, and, as she vanished, sweetly smiled.

Then Martin thrilled with solemn joy. Upon the sacred page read
    he:
"Hungry was I, ye gave me meat; thirsty, and ye gave drink to me;
A stranger I, ye took me in, and as unto the lowliest one
Of these my brethren, even the least, ye did it, unto Me 'twas done."

And Martin understood at last it was no vision born of sleep,
And all his soul in prayer and praise filled with a rapture still and
    deep.
He had not been deceived, it was no fancy of the twilight dim,
But glorious truth! The Master came, and he had ministered to
    Him.

# SEASIDE FLOWERS

ALONG the brim of the curving cove the small blue skull cap sits,
Where the grey beach bird, with happy cry, in safety feeds and flits,
And spreads or shuts the pimpernel its drowsy buds to tell
When rain will come, or skies will clear, the pretty pimpernel!
And the pink herbrobert all the day holds up its rosy flowers,
While high above with a purple plume the lofty thistle towers,
And the golden potentilla blows, and the crow foot laughs in the
    sun,
And over rock and bush and turf wild morning glories run.
They look down o'er the tiny cove, out to the blue, blue sea,
Neighbors and friends, all beautiful, a joyful company;
And when the tide comes brimming in with soft and gentle rush
It is as if the murmuring sound said to the silence, "Hush!"
All down the narrow beach the lilac mussel shells are strown
Among the scattered pebbles, and by the polished stone
Where the sea's hands have worn the ledge till smooth as ivory
O such a place on summer days to put your cheek, and lie
Listening to all the whispering waves that round the point go by!
For the sun has warmed the hard cold rock till it almost human
    seems,
And such a pillow as it makes for childhood's blissful dreams!
The little glad, caressing waves! They bring their treasure gay
To deck the lovely quiet beach, nor fail day after day
To strew the slope with crimson dulse and olive seaweed sprays,
And lace-like empty urchin shells, all rahgh with dull green rays,
The limpet's hollow, mottled house, and amber snail shells bright,
And brown and shining ruffled kelps and cockles, snowy white.
O such a happy, happy world! Were I to talk all day,
Not half the joy of that sweet spot could I begin to say!
And all the charming band of flowers that wakh the sea and sky,
They seem to know and love the winds that gently pass them by:
They seem to feel the freshnes of the waves at every tide
As they cross the quiet water that sparkles far and wide.

The bright sails go and come at will, the white gulls float in air,
The song sparrow and sandpiper are flitting, everywhere,
But the dark blue skull cap never sighs to leave its pleasant home,
With butterfly, or thistle-down, or sandpiper to roam,
The pink herbrobert nestles close, content in sun or rain,
Nor envies the white far sails that glide across the ocean plain;
The golden potentilla sees the soaring gull on high
Yet never does she wish for wings to join him in the sky,
For all these wise and lovely lives accord with God's intent,
Each takes its lot and bears its bloom as kindly nature meant.
Whatever weather fortune sends, they greet it patiently,
Each only striving its own way a perfect thing to be.
O tell me, little children, have you on summer days
Heard what the winds are whispering and what the water says?
The small birds' chirp, the cry of gulls, the crickets' quiet creak:—
And have you seen the charming things that have no power to speak,
The dear, sweet humble little flowers that all so silently
Teach such a lovely lesson every day, to you and me?
Go seek them, if you know them not, when summer comes once
    more
You'll find a pleasure in them you never knew before!

# FROM
*STORIES AND POEMS*
*FOR CHILDREN*

*Celia Thaxter with her grandson Charles Eliot in 1888 on
the piazza of her Appledore cottage.*

# GRANDMOTHER TO HER GRANDSON

OH, what are all life's treasures worth
    Compared to this love and its sweet surprise,
My little heaven upon the earth,
    With your pale gold hair and your serious eyes!

Who could have dreamed that a joy like this
    Lay in wait on life's downward slope,
To flood the heart with a freshet of bliss,
    And brighten eve with the morning's hope!

How dear the sound of the little feet,
    And the clasp of the little hand how dear.
And the little voice that falls so sweet,
    Like trilling music upon my ear!

Oh, to shield you from all life's harms,
    My fair white lamb with the innocent eyes,
To gather you close in my loving arms
    Safe from the frown of the lowering skies!

But into the wide world you must go
    From home's soft nest and its shelter warm,
Sorrow to meet and care to know
    In ways that are rough and dark with storm.

Heaven be good to you, dearest one!
    Help you to fight all the powers of ill,
Through life's long day to its setting sun
    Keep you God's soldier conquering still.

## THE WATER-BLOOM

A CHILD looked up in the summer sky
Where a soft, bright shower had just passed by;
Eastward the dusk rain-curtain hung,
And swiftly across it the rainbow sprung.

"Papa! Papa! what is it?" she cried,
As she gazed with her blue eyes opened wide
At the wonderful arch that bridged the heaven,
Vividly glowing with colors seven.

Why, that is the rainbow, darling child,"
And the father down on his baby smiled.
What makes it, papa?" "The sun, my dear,
That shines on the water-drops so clear."

Here was a beautiful mystery!
No more questions to ask had she,
But she thought the garden's loveliest flowers
Had floated upward and caught in the showers—

Rose, violet, orange marigold—
In a ribbon of light on the clouds unrolled!
Red of poppy, and green leaves too,
Sunflower yellow, and larkspur blue.

A great, wide, wondrous, splendid wreath
It seemed to the little girl beneath;
How did it grow so fast up there,
And suddenly blossom, high in the air?

She could not take her eyes from the sight:
Oh, look! " she cried in her deep delight,
As she watched the glory spanning the gloom,
"Oh, look at the beautiful water-bloom!"

# CROCUS

OH, the dear, delightful sound
Of the drops that to the ground
From the eaves rejoicing run
In the February sun!
Drip, drip, drip, they slide and slip
From the icicles' bright tip,
Till they melt the sullen snow
On the garden bed below.
"Bless me! what is all this drumming?"
Cries the crocus, "I am coming!
Pray don't knock me long and loud,
For I'm neither cross nor proud.
But a little sleepy still,
With the winter's lingering chill.
Never mind! 'Tis time to wake,
Through the dream at last to break!"
'T'is as quickly done as said;
Up she thrusts her golden head,
Looks about with radiant eyes
In a kind of shy surprise,
Tries to say in accents surly,
"Well! you called me very early!"
But she lights with such a smile
All the darksome place the while,
Every heart begins to stir
Joyfully at sight of her;
Every creature grows more gay
Looking in her face to-day.
She is greeted, "Welcome, dear!
Fresh smile of the hopeful year!
First bright print of Spring's light feet,
Golden crocus, welcome, sweet!"
And she whispers, looking up

285

From her richly glowing cup,
At the sunny eaves so high
Overhead against the sky,
"Now I've come, O sparkling drops,
All your clattering, pattering stops.
And I'm very glad I came,
And you're not the least to blame
That you hammered at the snow
Till you wakened me below
With your one incessant tune.
I'm not here a bit too soon!"

# MILKING

LITTLE dun cow to the apple-tree tied,
    Chewing the cud of reflection,
I that am milking you, sit by your side,
    Lost in a sad retrospection.

Far o'er the field the tall daisies blush warm,
    For rosy the sunset is dying;
Across the still valley, o'er meadow and farm,
    The flush of its beauty is lying.

White foams the milk in the pail at my feet,
    Clearly the robins are calling;
Soft blows the evening wind after the heat,
    Cool the long shadows are falling.

Little dun cow, 'tis so tranquil and sweet!
    Are you light-hearted, I wonder?
What do *you* think about,— something to eat?
    On clover and grass do you ponder?

I am remembering days that are dead,
    And a brown little maid in the gloaming,
Milking her cow, with the west burning red
    Over waves that about her were foaming.

Up from the sad east the deep shadows gloomed
    Out of the distance and found her;
Lightly she sang while the solemn sea boomed
    Like a great organ around her.

Under the light-house no sweet-brier grew,
    Dry was the grass, and no daisies
Waved in the wind, and the flowers were few
    That lifted their delicate faces.

But oh, she was happy, and careless, and blest,
    Full of the song sparrow's spirit;
Grateful for life, for the least and the best
    Of the blessings that mortals inherit.

Fairer than gardens of Paradise seemed
    The desolate spaces of water;
Nature was hers,— clouds that frowned— stars that gleamed,—
    What beautiful lessons they taught her!

Would I could find you again, little maid,
    Striving with utmost endeavor,—
Could find in my breast that light heart, unafraid,
    That has vanished for ever and ever!

# YELLOW-BIRD

YELLOW-BIRD, where did you learn that song,
    Perched on the trellis where grapevines clamber,
In and out fluttering, all day long,
    With your golden breast bedropped with amber?

Where do you hide such a store of delight,
    O delicate creature, tiny and slender,
Like a mellow morning sunbeam bright
    And overflowing with music tender!

You never learned it at all, the song
    Springs from your heart in rich completeness,
Beautiful, blissful, clear and strong,
    Steeped in the summer's ripest sweetness.

To think we are neighbors of yours! How fine!
    Oh, what a pleasure to watch you together,
Bringing your fern-down and floss to reline
    The nest worn thin by the winter weather!

Send up your full notes like worshipful prayers;
    Yellow-bird, sing while the summer's before you;
Little you dream that, in spite of their cares,
    Here's a whole family, proud to adore you!

# SLUMBER SONG

Thou little child, with tender, clinging arms,
  Drop thy sweet head, my darling, down and rest
Upon my shoulder, rest with all thy charms;
  Be soothed and comforted, be loved and blessed.

Against thy silken, honey-colored hair
  I lean a loving cheek, a mute caress;
Close, close I gather thee and kiss thy fair
  White eyelids, sleep so softly doth oppress.

Dear little face, that lies in calm content
  Within the gracious hollow that God made
In every human shoulder, where He meant
  Some tired head for comfort should be laid!

Most like a heavy-folded rose thou art,
  In summer air reposing, warm and still.
Dream thy sweet dreams upon my quiet heart,
  I watch thy slumber; naught shall do thee ill.

# THE BUTCHER-BIRD

I 'LL tell you a story, children,
    The saddest you ever heard,
About Rupert, the pet canary,
    And a terrible butcher-bird.

There was such a blinding snowstorm
    One could not see at all,
And all day long the children
    Had watched the white flakes fall;

And when the eldest brothers
    Had kissed mamma good-night,
And up the stairs together
    Had gone with their bedroom light,

Of a sudden their two fresh voices
    Rang out in a quick surprise,
Mamma! Papa! come quickly
    And catch him before he flies!"

On a picture-frame perched lightly,
    With his head beneath his wing,
They had found a gray bird sitting;
    That was a curious thing!

Downstairs to the cosy parlor
    They brought him, glad to find
For the storm-tossed wanderer shelter;
    Not knowing his cruel mind!

And full of joy were the children
    To think he was safe and warm,
And had chosen their house for safety

To hide from the raging storm!
"He shall stay with the pretty Rupert,
   And live among mother's flowers,
And he'll sing with our robin and sparrow;"
   And they talked about it for hours.

Alas, in the early morning
   There rose a wail and a cry,
And a fluttering wild in the cages,
   And Rupert's voice rang high.

We rushed to the rescue swiftly;
   Too late! On the shining cage,
The home of the happy Rupert,
   All rough with fury and rage,

Stood the handsome, horrible stranger,
   With black and flashing eye,
And torn almost to pieces
   Did poor dead Rupert lie!

Oh, sad was all the household,
   And we mourned for Rupert long.
The fierce wild shrike was prisoned
   In a cage both dark and strong.

And would you like, O children,
   His final fate to know
To Agassiz's Museum
   That pirate bird did go!

# DUST

HERE is a problem, a wonder for all to see.
    Look at this marvelous thing I hold in my hand!
This is a magic surprising, a mystery
    Strange as a miracle, harder to understand.

What is it? Only a handful of earth: to your touch
    A dry rough powder you trample beneath your feet,
Dark and lifeless; but think for a moment, how much
    It hides and holds that is beautiful, bitter, or sweet.

Think of the glory of color! The red of the rose,
    Green of the myriad leaves and the fields of grass,
Yellow as bright as the sun where the daffodil blows,
    Purple where violets nod as the breezes pass.

Think of the manifold form, of the oak and the vine,
    Nut, and fruit, and cluster, and ears of corn;
Of the anchored water-lily, a thing divine,
    Unfolding its dazzling snow to the kiss of morn.

Think of the delicate perfumes borne on the gale,
    Of the golden willow catkin's odor of spring,
Of the breath of the rich narcissus waxen-pale,
    Of the sweet pea's flight of flowers, of the nettle's sting.

Strange that this lifeless thing gives vine, flower, tree
    Color and shape and character, fragrance too;
That the timber that builds the house, the ship for the sea,
    Out of this powder its strength and its toughness drew!

That the cocoa among the palms should suck its milk
    From this dry dust, while dates from the self-same soil
Summon their sweet rich fruit: that our shining silk

The mulberry leaves should yield to the worm's slow toil.
How should the poppy steal sleep from the very source
    That grants to the grapevine juice that can madden or cheer?
How does the weed find food for its fabric coarse
    Where the lilies proud their blossoms pure uprear?

Who shall compass or fathom God's thought profound?
    We can but praise, for we may not understand;
But there's no more beautiful riddle the whole world round
    Than is hid in this heap of dust I hold in my hand.

## BLUEBIRDS IN AUTUMN

THIS morning.was gray and cloudy,
    And over the fading land
Autumn was casting the withered leaves
    Abroad with a lavish hand.

Sad lay the tawny pastures;
    Where the grass was brown and dry;
And the far-off hills were blurred with mist,
    Under the sombre sky.

The frost already had fallen,
    No bird seemed left to sing;
And I sighed to think of the tempests
    Between us and the spring.

But the woodbine yet was scarlet
    Where it found a place to cling;
And the old dead weeping-willow
    Was draped like a splendid king.

Suddenly out of the heavens,
　　Like sapphire sparks of light,
A flock of bluebirds swept and lit
　　In the woodbine garlands bright.

The tree was alive in a moment
　　With motion, color, and song;
How gorgeous the flash of their azure wings
　　The blood-red leaves among!

Beautiful, brilliant creatures!
　　What sudden delight they brought
Into the pallid morning,
　　Rebuking my dreary thought!

Only a few days longer,
　　And they would have flown, to find
The wonderful, vanished summer,
　　Leaving darkness and cold behind.

Oh, to flee from the bitter weather,
　　The winter's buffets and shocks,—
To borrow their strong, light pinions,
　　And follow their shining flocks!

While they sought for the purple berries,
　　So eager and bright and glad,
I watched them, dreaming of April,
　　Ashamed to have been so sad.

And I thought, "Though I cannot follow them,
　　I can patiently endure,
And make the best of the snowstorms,
　　And that is something more.

"And when I see them returning,
  All heaven to earth they'll bring;
And my joy will be the deeper,
  For I shall have earned the spring."

# UNDER THE LIGHT-HOUSE

BENEATH the tall, white light-house strayed the children,
  In the May morning sweet;
About the steep and rough gray rocks they wandered
  With hesitating feet;
For scattered far and wide the birds were lying,
  Quiet, and cold, and dead,
That met, while they were swiftly winging northward,
  The fierce light overhead;
And as the frail moths in the summer evenings
  Fly to the candle's blaze,
Rushed wildly at the splendor, finding only
  Death in those blinding rays.
And here were bobolink, and wren, and sparrow,
  Veery, and oriole,
And purple finch, and rosy grosbeak, swallows,
  And kingbirds quaint and droll;
Gay soldier blackbirds, wearing on their shoulders
  Red, gold-edged epaulets,
And many a homely brown, red-breasted robin,
  Whose voice no child forgets.
And yellow-birds— what shapes of perfect beauty!
  What silence after song!
And mingled with them, unfamiliar warblers
  That to far woods belong.
Clothing the gray rocks with a mournful beauty
  By scores the dead forms lay,
That, dashed against the tall tower's cruel windows,
  Dropped like the spent sea spray.

How many an old and sun-steeped barn, far inland,
    Should miss about its eaves
The twitter and the gleam of these swift swallows!
    And, swinging 'mid the leaves,
The oriole's nest, all empty in the elm-tree,
    Would cold and silent be,
And nevermore these robins make the meadows
    Ring with their ecstasy.
Would not the gay swamp-border miss the blackbirds,
    Whistling so loud and clear?
Would not the bobolinks' delicious music
    Lose something of its cheer?
"Yet," thought the wistful children, gazing landward,
    "The birds will not be missed;
Others will take their place in field and forest,
    Others will keep their tryst:
And we, we only, know how death has met them;
    We wonder and we mourn
That from their innocent and bright existence
    Thus roughly they are torn."
And so they laid the sweet, dead shapes together,
    Smoothing each ruffled wing,
Perplexed and sorrowful, and pondering deeply
    The meaning of this thing.
(Too hard to fathom for the wisest nature
    Crowned with the snows of age!)
And all the beauty of the fair May morning
    Seemed like a blotted page.
They bore them down from the rough cliffs of granite
    To where the grass grew green,
And laid them 'neath the soft turf, all together,
    With many a flower between;
And, looking up with wet eyes, saw how brightly
    Upon the summer sea
Lay the clear sunlight, how white sails were shining,
    And small waves laughed in glee:

And somehow, comfort grew to check their grieving,
    A sense of brooding care,
As if, in spite of death, a loving presence
    Filled all the viewless air.
"What should we fear?" whispered the little children,
    "There is no thing so small
But God will care for it in earth or heaven:
    He sees the sparrows fall!"

## THE FLOCK OF DOVES

THE world was like a wilderness
    Of soft and downy snow;
The trees were plumed with feathery flakes,
    And the ground was white below.

Came the little mother out to the gate
    To watch for her children three;
Her hood was red as a poppy-flower,
    And rosy and young was she.

She took the snow in her cunning hands,
    As waiting she stood alone,
And lo! in a moment, beneath her touch,
    A fair white dove had grown.

A flock she wrought, and on the fence
    Set them in bright array,
With folded wings, or pinions spread,
    Ready to fly away.

And then she hid by the pine-tree tall,
    For the children's tones rang sweet,
As home from school, through the drifts so light,
    They sped with merry feet.

"O Nannie, Nannie! See the fence
    Alive with doves so white!"
"Oh, hush! don't frighten them away!"
    They whisper with delight.

They crept so soft, they crept so still,
    The wondrous sight to see,'
The little mother pushed the gate,
    And laughed out joyfully.

She clasped them close, she kissed their cheeks,
    And lips so sweet and red.
"The birds are only made of snow!
    You are my doves," she said.

## A POPPY SEED

"TELL you a story," my beautiful dear,
    "Of nixies, and pixies, and fairies with wings?"
Well, curl up close in the corner here,
    And I'll show you more astonishing things!

I give you this small white packet to hold.
    "It rustles," you say. Both the ends are sealed.
Patience a moment, and you shall be told
    Of the hundreds of captives that lie concealed

In this little paper. "What, living things?"
    Yes, full of life. "Won't I take one out?"
Yes, only be careful,—they have no wings,
    But your lightest breathing will blow them about.

There, one in your warm pink palm I lay:
    You hardly can see it! "Does anything hide
In that wee atom of dust?" you say.

Yes, wonderful glory is folded inside!

Robes, my dear, that are fit for kings;
    Scarlet splendor that dazzles the eyes;
Buds, flowers, leaves, stalks,— so many things!
    You look in my face with doubting surprise,

And ask, "Is it really, truly true?"
    No fairy story at all this time!
Don't you remember the poppy that grew
    At the foot of the trellis where sweet peas climb,

Last summer, close to the doorstep, where
    You and I loved to sit in the sun,
And see the butterflies float in the air
    When the long bright day was almost done?

Don't you remember what joy we had
    Watching that poppy grow high and higher,
In its lovely gray-green garments clad,
    Till the buds one evening showed streaks of fire,

And next day—oh! it was all ablaze;
    Three or four flowers at once outburst
In the early sun's low, golden rays—
    And you were down at the doorstep first—

And what magnificence met our sight!
    What a heavenly time we had, we two,
Just adoring it, lost in delight!
    For the gray-green leaves were spangled with dew,

And the flowers, like banners of silken flame
    Unfurled, stood each on its slender stem,
While the soft breeze over them went and came,
    Lightly and tenderly rocking them.

Dearest, don't you remember it all?
    How still it was! Not a whisper of sound,
Till a bird sang out from the garden wall,
    And you slid from the step and stood on the ground,

And the poppy was higher than your bright head!
    Gently downward one flower you bent
To see in the midst of its burning red
    The delicate greens in a glory blent.

Bronze-green pollen on glowing rays
    From a centre of palest emerald light
In a brilliant halo beneath our gaze,—
    You haven't forgotten that exquisite sight?

No, indeed! I was sure of it! Well,
    All that perfection of shape and hue,
That wealth of beauty no tongue can tell,
    Lies hid in this seed I have given to you.

Just such a speck in the friendly ground
    I planted last May by the doorstep wide;
The selfsame marvel that then we found
    This atom of dust holds shut inside.

You can't believe it I But all are there,—
    Leaves, roots, flowers, stalks, color, and glow;
Tell me a story that can compare
    With this for a wonder, if any you know!

# SPRING PLANTING-TIME

WHAT will you sow, little children, what will you sow?
In your garden you wish that sweet flowers would blossom and
    grow!
Then be careful to choose from the myriads of wonderful seeds
The caskets that lock up delight, and beware of the weeds!

If you sow nettles, alas for the crop you will reap!
Stings and poison and pain, bitter tears for your eyes to weep.
If you plant lilies and roses and pinks and sweet peas
What beauty will charm you, what perfumes on every breeze!

Thus will it be, little folk, in the garden of life;
Sow seeds of ill-nature, you'll reap only sorrow and strife;
But pleasant, kind words, gentle deeds, happy thoughts if you sow,
What roses and lilies of love will spring round you and grow!

Smiles will respond to yours, brighter than marigolds are,
And sweeter than fragrance of any sweet flowers, by far;
From the blossoms of beautiful deeds will a blessing arise,
And a welcome at sight of you kindle in every one's eyes.

Then what will you sow, my dear children, what will you sow?
Seeds of kindness, of sweetness, of patience, drop softly, and lo!
Love shall blossom around you in joy and in beauty, and make
A garden of Paradise here upon earth for your sake.

# THE SPRAY SPRITE

ONCE upon a time, a thousand years ago, there dwelt by the sea a little maid. Had I said in the sea, it would perhaps have been as well, for such a spray sprite never danced before at a breaker's edge. It was bliss to her to watch that great sea, to hear its sweet or awful voices, to feel the salt wind lift her thick brown hair and kiss her cheek; to wade, bare-footed, into the singing, sparkling brine. Above all things, she hated to sew patchwork. Oh, but she was a naughty child,—not at all like the good, decorous little girls who will perhaps read this story. She didn't like to sweep and dust, and keep all things bright and tidy. She wished to splash in the water the whole day long, and dance, and sing, and string shells, and be idle like the lovely white kittiwakes that flew to and fro above her, and came at the beckoning of her hand. She looked with scorn on dolls and all their appointments and never wished to play with them,— it was almost as bad as patchwork! But she loved the sky, and all the clouds and stars, the sun that made a glory in the east and west at morning and evening, the changing moon, the streaming Northern Lights. The winds seemed human, so much they had to say to her. She thought, "The north wind fights me; the west wind plays with me; the east wind sighs, and is always ready to weep; the south wind loves and kisses me." Every wave that whitened the face of the vast sea was dear to her; every bird that floated over, every sail that glided across,—all brought her a thrill of joy. And what a wild and keen delight came to her with the thunder, lightning, and the rain!—but with all her heart she hated the cold, white snow. Much she liked to creep out of the house in the dusk of dawn and climb the highest rocks to see the morning break. Wrapping herself close from the chill wind, curling into a niche of the rough granite cliff, how beautiful it was, all alone with the soaring gulls, to watch the east grow rosy, rosier to the very zenith, till she shouted with joy,

302

facing the uprisen sun! Then it was so splendid to stand on the rocks when the billows came stumbling in, sending the spray flying high in the air, and throwing handfuls of crimson dulse at her, or long brown tresses of seaweed, which she caught and flung back again, while she was drenched with the shower, and the wind blew her about in rough play. And blissful it was to run with the sandpipers along the edge of the shallow waves on the little beach, and dance in the clear green water; or, at low tide, to hang over the still surface of pools among the rocks, wherein lay treasures untold.

Oh, those gardens of the sea! Who shall describe their beauty? It was as if a piece of rainbow had fallen and melted into them, such myriads of many-colored creatures and plants inhabited them. Dear children, if I were to talk to you the whole day, I could not tell you half the wonderful things she saw in those clear depths. But I think she liked best of them all the dainty Eolis, a delicate shell-less snail, with rosy spines and tiny horns.

To watch all this marvelous life at the edge of the wild ocean was enchanting, and she never wearied of it. Then, among the higher rocks, grew a few land plants and grasses, and a single root of fern, a world of delight to her; a whole tropical forest would not have been so precious. She gathered plumes of the bright goldenrod that nodded in the clefts, and crowned herself with long garlands of the wild pink morning-glory; and the gulls and the sandpipers looked at her, and wondered, I dare say, what she did it for;—they could have told quite as well as she. To the little pimpernel, always ready to shut its scarlet flowers at the slightest shadow of a cloud, she said: " I love you pimpernel, for you're always dreaming, and that's what I like to do." And so she did dream, and with the everlasting sound of the her in her ears, I wonder she ever believed anything to be real!

She was a very happy little maid and perfectly content, but still she could not help longing to know what lay beyond the round horizon that hemmed her in with the waves, and many and many a day, rocking in her little boat on the tranquil water, she gazed at the dim linc where the sky seemed to rest on the sea, and pondered until she was lost in a maze of aimless thought."

Over there, beyond the faint blue cloud of distant coast, lies the great world," she said. "Is it beautiful there?" Sometimes at sunrise it looked most beautiful, flushed with delicious color,—purple, and rose, and gold. Vessels glided by, hither and thither, at all times of the day and night. Whence came they? Whither did they go? If, in the morning sunshine, she saw the shadow of one sail fall upon another, as some craft passed near, the sight made this little savage happy, that it was better than if she had found a mine of gold,—the foolish thing to be happy at a shadow!

She laughed and talked with the loons, and learned to imitate their weird wild cry; she stretched her arms up to the big burgomaster gull flying over, crying, "Take me to ride with you, burgomaster, between your broad wings!" Driftwood came sailing to the shore, bits of bark,—on what tree did they grow she wondered. Pieces of oars,— who had paddled with them? Laths, sticks, straws, blocks, logs, branches, cones, tangled with ribbon-grass kelp and rock-weed,— each thing had a history if she did but know it, she thought. Sometimes came a green fir bough; there was a wonder, for no trees grew among her rocks, there was not soil enough to hold their roots. Sometimes she came upon tokens of wreck and disaster that made her heart shrink, for she did not like to think that pain was in this lovely world wherein she was so glad to be alive.

But she always fancied she should find some strange and costly thing as she sought among the weeds and drift, —that some mysterious and beautiful thing would come floating across the sea for her, among the odds and ends, one day, and something did come, as you shall hear.

One night she was playing on the beach alone; she gathered shells and seaweeds; full of joy, she laughed and sang to herself. It was high tide and sunset; all the west was red and clear; a golden glory lay along the calm water from the sinking sun to her feet, as she stood at the edge of the tide. Near by, the lighthouse began to twinkle in crimson and gold; far off, large vessels, with their sails full of the twilight, passed by, silent and slow. The waves made a continual talking among themselves, and sweet and disconsolate came the cry of the sandpipers along the shore. All else was very still. She stopped her play and sat down on a rock, and let her bare feet drop within reach of the water, while she watched the gulls slowly floating home, by twos and threes, through the lovely evening sky. She smiled to see them beat the air with their wide wings, with a slow and measured motion. She knew where their lonesome rock lay, far out on the eastern sea.

By and by all were gone; the red faded, but a pure and peaceful light still held the west, and the stars came out one after one. She sat still there a long time; the warm wind wrapped her close, she felt no chill with the falling dew. Wistfully peering out toward the horizon-line, she did not for some time notice that the sea was full of cool fire, "sparks that snap and burst and flee;" every wave left its outline in vanishing gold on the wet weeds and sand; her feet were covered; it was as if she had on golden-spangled slippers. That was charming! The tide had begun to fall now, and left bare a gray rock worn and polished by the waves—heaven knows how many thousands of years!—till it was as smooth as satin. She laid her cheek against it, the dear old gray rock! It was her pet pillow. Though the water had just flowed over it, it was warm yet from the sun which had blazed down all the long clear summer day. Then she watched the pale flame glow-ing, and fading, and glowing again, till— Well, I never could be quite sure how much of what I am going to tell you she dreamed, and how much really happened, but the main points are certainly true.

After she had been watching and listening a while, she became aware of an unaccustomed sound among the noises of the washing tide and whispers of the wind. Presently she perceived, between the tide-mark and the ebbing water, two dim, slender figures busy among the weeds, and sweet, clear voices reached her with a merry mingling of talk and laughter. The figures drew near,—a youth, dark and brilliant, a maiden, bright and fair. They were filling little baskets with the phosphorescent sparks, and ever. spark they touched became a permanent star, so that the little baskets were overflowing with the harmless flame. She could not comprehend their talk, but she watched them eagerly. The youth dipped his finger into the pale fire, and touched with it the girl's white forehead and left there a spark that flickered upward, then, brightened and stood steady, a glittering star, so beautiful above her dusky hair! And the child saw the fairy maiden blush as she swung the basket lightly to her shoulder. She rose up as they turned, and confronted, them, and both sprang toward her. "Child of the spray," they cried, "it is thyself we came to seek;" and grasping her hands, they drew her gently after them into a small, lonely cove, where the water lay like a mirror, with all the stars in heaven shining out of it.

And by the starlight what an enchanting sight she saw! Moored close to the beach, a fairy fleet was waiting motionless,—seven great purple mussel-shells as large as her own little skiff, each lined with mother-of-pearl, and strewn with silken cushions; in each a tapering mast, from which drooped lightly down the idle sail, shining like silver, bright as if woven of thistle-down. And at each curling prow was set a cluster of phosphorescent stars, gleaming and never disappearing, and every boat had its merry crew of fairy creatures, and in the midst, alone in his skiff, sat a fairy prince with a golden crown. When they saw their comrades bringing the spray child, they set up a sweet outcry, and pushed the boats ashore with slender oars, and leaped out and danced about her. Was she awake or asleep? The tide had fallen farther yet. A large purple starfish glided on the sand and paused close by. Many-hued little shells crept near and listened, and pearly Eolis, from a crystal pool at hand, lifted her crested head to listen also. The child rubbed her eyes, and looked about on every side,—the sand was real beneath her feet, the familiar sound of the water was surely in her ears, there were the stars above burning steadily. She was awake, she thought, though it was night; but when she looked at the fairy prince, she thought it was sunrise suddenly. He came near and took her hand, and as he did so all the sandpipers cried aloud in their dreams, and made their playmate tremble with mournful foreboding.

"Come," he said, "I have sailed across the sea, to show you what lies beyond the wonderful horizon. Come with me;" and without knowing how, she was sitting in the beautiful boat by his side, and all the fairy creatures were busy casting off the ropes, and trimming the sails, with song and shout, and as swiftly those shimmering sails ran up to the tops of the delicate masts, the south wind filled them; sudden wafts of music, fine and sweet, rose and fell, and out of the little cove swept the fleet of shells, rustling canvas, gleaming stars, and brilliant faces, and all. Rapidly they passed from sight, and then on the lonely beach, the sandpipers cried more disconsolately, and the waves broke ever with a lonelier sound, for nevermore came that little spray sprite back to play with them again.

What became of her! Well, that I will tell you also. At first, she was listening to such a wonderful story that she quite forgot everything else; but, as they sailed and sailed, one by one the fairy crews disappeared, and still little Idleness and the fairy prince sailed on and on, till at last they came to the great world which had looked so beautiful to the child's eyes from afar,—all gold, and pearl, and rose-color. And of what do you think she found it was made, after all? Why, my dear children, only patch work! Everybody was doing patchwork of one kind or another,—black patches and white, blue patches and gray,—and everybody was so busy that it was astonishing to witness. I do not mean to say that everybody was sewing with needle and thread, but all were at work upon something; and she comprehended that while she had been dancing in the spray, wiser children had been learning all kinds of useful things, of which she knew nothing at all, and how much time she had lost!

At first it was wearisome enough,—like living in a big ant-hill, with all the ants rushing about pell-mell. And then all the trees, hills, and fields seemed to be crowding up to the windows for the express purpose of smothering the poor mermaid. There wasn't half enough sky, and no water at all, to speak of; and everything was so stiff and still, except. the hurrying people. The trees waved, but they couldn't go sweeping off as the grand ships did over the sea, and as for the fields, they were well enough, but altogether too still; they never changed about like the shifting, musical, many-colored sea. And yet some of them were lovely, when the wind bowed all the tall white daisies toward her, like the crest of a breaking wave; better so than when they blushed with clover-bloom, or flamed in buttercups and dandelions. The brooks and rivers were good as far as they went, but there was so little of them! And if she liked the hills, it was because they seemed to her like huge, petrified waves, heaved solemnly against the sky. Alas for her great horizon! She pined for it night and day.

But gradually she began to get used to the tame life, and slowly, very slowly, she found out a secret worth all the beauty she had lost. As young people don't know it generally, I'll whisper it in your ear. This is it: that work is among the best blessings God, gave the world; that to be useful and helpful, even in the smallest ways, brings a better bliss than all the delightful things you can think of, put together. And this bliss is within the reach of every human being. She was glad when she found it out for herself. And so now she does patchwork, to the end of her days,— patchwork in this case meaning all kinds of work under the sun, a little here, and a little there. You would never know now that she had been a spray sprite, and danced among the breakers, and talked and laughed with the loons, for she is like everybody else, except that, sleeping or waking, year after year, she keeps in her ears the sad, mysterious murmur of the sea, just like a hollow shell.

# PEGGY'S GARDEN,
# AND WHAT GREW THEREIN

PEGGY! Peggy!" Who was calling Peggy? But the question seemed rather to be who was not calling her. From the corner by the low window came the grandmother's querulous voice, "Peggy, my dear, come and pick up my stitch! I've dropped a stitch, and my old eyes can't find it," and Peggy turned to her; but before she had straightened the knitting, a little voice rose in a wail from the door-step, where her small brother whittled a boat from a water-worn shingle, "Oh, Peggy, I've cut my finger! Oh, come, Peggy, bring a rag and do it up! " and mother by the cradle said, "Peggy, do take the baby a minute while I finish mixing the brown-bread."

Even outside the cottage door father was saying, "Peggy, dear, bring me a drink of water," as he tinkered his dory close by. She took the baby from her mother's arms and went to the woeful brother." Don't cry, Willy, dear, run to mother for a rag; wait a minute, please, father,"—and Willie having brought a little strip of cotton, she sat down on the doorstep and proceeded to bind the wounded finger while the baby lay cooing on her knees. "Now run, and take some water to father; there's a good boy," she said, as she wiped the tears away from two cheeks like apples, round and rosy. And Willy scampered for the dipper, and carried it dripping to his father, and then returned to nestle close to his sister's side. The baby fretted a little, and Peggy gathered it up and laid its pretty head tenderly against her shoulder and crooned to it soft and low:—

*There was a ship a-sailing, a-sailing on the sea.*
*And oh! it was all laden with pretty things for thee!*

till it opened its large wise eyes and gazed out at the glitter and sparkle of the bright day, and tried to find its mouth with its thumb in an aimless but contented fashion.

"Sing the rest of it, sister," begged Willy.

There was a world of love in the little fellow's gesture as he slipped both hands around Peggy's arm and hugged it tight while she went on:—

*There were comfits in the cabin and apples in the hold,*
*The sails were made of silk and the masts were made of gold:*
*The four-and-twenty sailors that walked about the decks*
*Were four-and-twenty white mice with chains about their necks;*
*The captain was a duck with a compass on his back,*
*And when the ship began to sail, the captain cried, 'quack, quack!'*

"Now sing it all over again!" cried Willy, laying his cheek against the arm he was hugging; "do please sing it all over again! " And laughing, patient Peggy began it again.

There was a porch outside the door, and the shadow of its square roof fell on the wooden step where the children sat. There were vines of flowering-bean and morning-glory trained up at the sides, all blossoming in scarlet clusters and deep blue bells.

It was a hot, bright July day. Before the cottage stretched the level beach of purplish-gray shimmering sand; and beyond it the summer sea, light turquoise blue and calm, lay smiling, streaked with lines of lazy foam from long-spent breakers far away. On a promonotory reaching to the east, the large mass of the buildings of a great hotel basked in the heat, its warmly tinted walls and red roofs dimly beautiful in the soft haze of the distance. The pine woods were thick behind the cottage and stretched away to the south; near it a patch of earth was devoted to "garden stuff,"—potatoes, beans, and the like, and beyond this was a flower-garden, so luxuriant and splendid in color that one wondered at seeing it in so poor a place.

Peggy's childish voice was very pleasant to hear as she sang to the children.

Her father and mother had given her the sweet and stately name of Margaret, but her grandmother had adopted its old-fashioned abbreviation of Peggy, and it had grown dear in all ears where she was known. She was a girl of about thirteen, not tall for her age, but slender, with rich, red-gold hair, which was a great cross and affliction to her; for every one who spoke of it did so in a half-pitying way, as if it were to be deprecated at least, if not a thing of which to be thoroughly ashamed. Such vigorous, rebellious hair, too, thronging back from her honest forehead in richly waved, thick locks, which no combing would make straight and smooth. How she envied the sleek, satin sheen of the heads of the few girls she knew! Her eyes were clear and gray, her mouth large, with fine and noble curves and even, white teeth, and her fresh cheek was touched by many salutations of the sun. No one would ever have called her pretty,—the word could not apply to her,—but there was an indescribable air of modesty and sweet intelligence about her which at once attracted and charmed.

The sunshine flickered through the leaves and touched her bright head as she sat with the little ones in the porch. Inside, the mother's swift step went to and fro, about her work; by the open window, the grandmother's knitting-needles clicked softly. Outside, there were the sounds of bees and early crickets, a bird's note now and then, the call of a sandpiper, the song of a sparrow, or a cry far aloft in the blue from a wandering gull afloat on white wings, ever the low, far murmuring of the sea, and again and again the dull strokes of the hammer with which the father was mending his boat. As he moved about, it was evident he was lame; a long sickness in the winter had left him "crippled," as his neighbors said, with rheumatism. He had a fine, intelligent face, and had not always lived the life which poverty now forced upon him. His eyes were sad and anxious, he looked weather-beaten and worn, and his expression enlisted one's sympathies at once. He was fighting a hard fight to keep the wolf from his door; for his lameness made it extremely difficult to go fishing, like the rest of the folk living near. And now, since the attack of illness had exhausted every resource, very slender at the best, he was worn with anxiety for the coming winter's necessities. In summer it was well enough; they could make a shift to live from day to day; but when every force of nature should be marshaled against them in the bitter weather to come, how would they be able to endure it, and fight want away till another spring? He hardly dared to think of it.

Peggy adored her father. She was his chief and best joy in the world. When she saw him so full of care, and heard him with the good and patient mother discussing ways and means of getting bread, when they dreamed not she was listening, she would have given worlds to help them. Her whole mind was full of the problem. What could she do? Leave them and go away and try to earn something to help? But they would not listen to it; they could not live without her. She was their courage, their stay, their joy, and cheer, embodied. One winter's day, when her father was at his worst, and she felt as though despair were settling down upon them, she remembered the groups of idle pleasure-seekers she had seen wandering across the sands in summer days, from the great hotel on the Point. "How wonderful must be their lives, with no anxieties like ours!" she thought.

As the picture of these loiterers lingered in her imagination, she remembered the flowers they wore, the buttonhole bouquets of the men, and the nosegays of the maidens, and like a flash it came to Peggy what she might do. She might have a garden of her own, and sell flowers to these people at the hotel,—why not? She would try, at least. She told her mother and father of her thought; but they did not give it much weight at first. Still she was not daunted. With a resolute energy she bent all powers to compass it. First, she chose a piece of ground wherein some former occupant of the place had raised vegetables; it was partly surrounded by a ruinous wall to keep out stray cattle, and was close under the southern windows of their rickety little cottage. There was not much snow upon the ground, and every day she went to the beach and brought basket after basket of kelp, which she spread upon the ground, till by patience and perseverance she had covered it all over. It was not an easy task, and she had driftwood to bring daily from the beach, beside. But she knew how much more hope of success she would have if only she could spread the seaweed and leave it to impart its nourishment to the sandy soil; and when it was done, she rejoiced in every rain that helped it to decay. The next thing was to get seeds for her garden. And when her father was better, so that she could be spared, she took long walks inland among their widely scattered neighbors to beg of each a few; for every house had its little flower-plot in summer; and the folk were kind and gave her all they could spare, marigolds, larkspur, sweet peas and mignonette, sunflowers, nasturtiums, pansies, and coreopsis, hardy, humble flowers, friendly and swift to grow.

"I'm sure you're welcome to 'em, child," Aunt Sally, the blacksmith's wife, had said, as she put the packet into Peggy's hand; "and I hope ye'll do all you're thinkin' to with 'em; but I calc'late ye have no idea what a job 'tis to take care on 'em," a fact which Peggy did indeed discover in good time. "If ye'll come up in the spring, I'll give ye a root o' lad's love and lemon-balm; they smell very sweet an' pure, but they don't have any seeds to speak on," the old lady added.

With what anxious joy Peggy watched for the first signs of spring! As soon as the snow was melted, she began to work about her garden-plot, every day a little, as long as she could be spared. With her strong young arms she brought stone by stone to the broken wall till she had made it whole again; but it was a work of days and weeks. Then little by little she raked away the kelp. But the most difficult part of the work was to come, to dig up the earth thoroughly, "could she do it?" she wondered. Here came an unexpected help. One day a neighbor with spritsail spread to the breeze, flying past at high tide, came so near that he made out what Peggy was trying to do in her walled inclosure.

"Wal, if that don't beat all!" he said to himself; "if there isn't Maxwell's red-haired gal tryin' to dig a garden! Her father's laid up, blest if she hasn't spunk!" That night, after supper, he walked down from "his place" and presented himself with a broad spade in his hand. "Why couldn't ye have asked some on us to help ye?" he cried, with rough kindness; and straightway set himself to work with such a will that before dark it was all done, nor would he listen to her thanks as he went off. "I wish ye good luck with your garden!" he said, and so departed, followed by Peggy's gratitude.

There was yet much work to be done, but she could do it all, she knew, and she toiled away with a light heart, till she had raked out every stone and laid the beds all straight and even, and planted every seed; and then she paused to rest. By this time her father was able to creep about a little, for the days were growing long, and he looked at Peggy's handiwork with tears in his eyes. He was too helpless to do much to the little patch where every year he tried to raise a few vegetables, so Peggy put her young shoulder to that wheel also, and planted the beans and potatoes, and gave them all the care she could. Meantime she rejoiced in the fresh showers which fell to moisten the hidden flower-seeds, and the warm sun which would coax the green leaves from the dark earth. Every turn of weather had a new interest for her, every hour was bright with hope. "I declare," said the grandmother, "it does me good just to see the child; she's brighter than a summer mornin'!"

Indeed she was, so full of cheer, so modest, dutiful, and patient, the kindest little heart that ever beat in human breast, always ready to help and comfort wherever comfort was needed! Happy girl! Her gentle nature was a key that all unconsciously to herself opened for her rich treasures of love that should not fail.

One morning in the last week in May, small Willy came running in quite breathless. "Peggy, come out and look! The seeds have comed up all in a row, like little green soldiers!" And Peggy, with the baby on her arm, followed the delighted little fellow to the garden. It was true, at last; there were rows of corn-flowers and marigolds piercing the soil, the first and strongest of them all. And after them, day after day, came the rest in a swift procession, till it seemed as if a soft green veil were laid over the earth. Then began work indeed, for with the flowers had spruug ten thousand weeds more vigorous than they. But there is no saying truer than that "where there's a will there's a way," and Peggy, not being able to get away from household cares during the day, would steal the hours from sleep to accomplish her object. It was light enough to see between three and four o'clock in the morning, and many and many a pink dawn found her kneeling on the dewy ground (whereon she had spread a bit of carpet, for she had been taught never to trifle with her health), weeding industriously, till there was not a green thing except the flowers to be seen in the whole place. no sooner were the weeds conquered, however, than they rose again, a second colony— clover, quitch-grass, purslane, chickweed, pigweed, ragweed, and the rest, and when these had been exterminated, then came transplanting, separating the crowded plants, putting sticks and strings along the wall for the vines to climb, and a tiresome, daily system of watering to be carried on, without which the whole attempt would have been a failure. Fortunately there was a fine well near the house, and even little Willie could help, and father could stand and pump for them, and sometimes bring water, too; and so at last the reward of so much toil and care was before them. The garden was truly a beautiful sight. Over the wall the nasturtiums ran like flame, and the sweet peas climbed, just breaking into white and pink and purple and wonderful scarlet, and the flowering bean clusters were almost as red as pomegranate blossoms. There were ranks of corn-flowers in lovely, delicate rose and azure; there were marigolds and venidiums, whole solar systems of suns and stars; there were golden summer chrysanthemums and *Coreopsis coronata* superb to see, and phloxes that were like masses of rich velvet-scarlet, maroon and pink and crimson. There were others to come, asters and zinnias and sunflowers later; but the mignonette had begun, and spikes of larkspur—

burning, brilliant blue— set off the yellow and fire colors, and the California poppies— cups of flaming gold—and the pied pansies, and crimson flax, and pink mallows! Well might the whole family wonder and rejoice over Peggy's garden, and all the neighbors make pilgrimages to see it!

And now at last it was time for the great attempt, and she was trying to summon all her courage to take on the morrow her first flowers to the hotel, for sale. A kind of stage fright came over the poor child at this eleventh hour. After all her brave toil, it would seem a simple thing to take her blossoms and pace quietly the long piazzas where wealth and beauty and idleness would give her the daily bread for herself and her dear ones in exchange. But the shy girl felt as if it were an absolute impossibility. Suddenly all her courage ebbed and left her in deep despondency. She sat by the little window in the grandmother's old chair; the wind that wandered through the beautiful summer twilight brought her the delicate sweet odors from her garden; their sweetness made her heart sink. She turned from the open casement. In the corner, by a dim little lamp, her mother was mending the worn sleeves of her father's coat. Peggy looked at her. How pale and patient she was! The cradle stood near, and her foot sought the rocker and stirred it gently each time the baby nestled uneasily; in the armchair near, her father had fallen asleep, his fine pathetic face faintly touched by the feeble light. His thin hand lay on the arm of the chair. How thin it was, how sad his sleeping face! Not one of them had quite all they needed to eat on that day; and what for to-morrow? Then a feeling of shame at her own cowardice came to Peggy's rescue. What were ten thousand indifferent eyes, what if everybody should laugh at her red hair and mean apparel; if they only would buy her flowers, she would not care, no, she would *not!* She would be deaf, dumb, and blind to everything except her purpose. She left the window and came and stood beside her mother's chair. "Mother, dear, let me finish it for you," she said, trying to take the work out of her hands. But her mother said, "No, Peggy, darling, don't mind, I've nearly finished. You'd better go to bed soon, for you'll have to be up very early, you know"; and she put her arm around her girl's slender figure and drew her close, and laid her tired head against the brave little heart that was beating fast with its struggles and hopes and fears. Her father opened his eyes upon the two, all unconscious of his gaze. No one knew better than he what was passing in his daughter's mind. But he had no word with which to comfort her; he could only cling to her as her mother was doing, and bless her with all his soul, as she came to give him a goodnight kiss.

She climbed to her little nest under the eaves and leaned out to look once more at the summer night. The calm sea mirrored every twinkling star. Here and there a light gleamed from some fishing-schooner anchored and rocking almost imperceptibly on the softly heaving tide. Afar on its lonely promontory stood the dark mass of the great hotel, ablaze and quivering with electric lights, like a living jewel of many facets. So great a hope, so great a fear for her trembled in its glitter and gleam. She was glad she could not hear the band that she knew must be playing for the gay, whirling dancers in the great hall. "I wonder if they all are wearing flowers from the city," she thought, "roses and delicate things so different from mine. I wonder if they will want mine when they see them! Perhaps, perhaps!" she sighed.

Little Willy was asleep in the low cot; he half woke as she laid her head on the pillow, and possessed himself of her arm, hugging it again with both his.

"Dear Peggy," he said, half asleep, "dear! dear, *dear!*"

The morning broke calm and clear. It was not four o'clock when she was stealing out in the freshening dawn to her garden-plot. The sky was one great flush of pink, and at the horizon crimson and gold where the sun approached from the other side and all the sea reflected the sky.

"Oh!" thought she "the whole world looks like a rose!" as she pushed the gate and entered the path. How the birds were singing! "Oh! song sparrow!" she cried to the little brown creature that sat on

317

the wall and poured forth such a strain of joy that it seemed to fill the air with cheer! "are you really so glad as that? I'd like to change places with you!"

She cut the flowers wish swift and dexterous hands, and filled her basket heaping full. And now the sun had risen in still magnificence, and touched with golden finger the sails of small fishing-craft, creeping out to the day's work, and the snowy wings of lazy gulls afloat overhead in the perfect blue, and made the bright hair of our Peggy as glorious as the marigolds she was tying into bunches as she sat on the little step with her basket and a spool of thread. Some dim artistic sense led her to mass each color separately. All the scarlet sweet peas she put together. So with the pink and the purple and the white; so with the red poppies, to which she added a few delicate grasses, and with the mignonette; but with the pale-yellow summer chrysanthemums she put a few orange marigolds, and made of their radiant disks a splendid conflagration of color. There were small and large bunches to be tied, and buttonhole bouquets; and when all were done, she put them into a wooden tub with a few inches of water, and left it in the cool dark of the cellar till she should be ready to take them away. But the slender breakfast was to be helped on and the family started for the day, before she could leave them. The baby, usually so good and quiet, *would* fret; it seemed to be out of sorts.

"Poor little girl," Peggy said to herself, "you are hungry; that is the trouble, I know, for you are best little sister in the world."

The grandmother was full of aches and pains this morning, but she said, "I'll keep the baby, Peggy, dear; you go and get ready before the sun grows so hot that you'll suffer going across the sands. Here's something to wear on your head, child," and she drew out of her pocket a nicely folded blue handkerchief; "it's better than nothing," she said, "though it's faded and old enough." Poor Peggy! She had no hat at all; the handkerchief was, as grandmother said, better than nothing,— that was all.

"Go, now, and walk very slowly, dear," her mother said. She

brought a long and broad shallow basket, into which they put the flowers, and over all laid lightly some newspapers, which were tucked carefully in around the edges, to save her treasures from wind and sun. She had but her one gown to wear, a dull, dark-blue cotton print, made in the simplest fashion, with neither frill nor fur below. She had no time for such, nor means if she had had time. Her thick, bright locks were plaited into one long, rich braid with the ends left loose, for she had not even a bit of ribbon wherewith to tie it. She knotted the blue kerchief under her chin, kissed them all as if she were bidding the family farewell for a month, and set off with her basket on her arm. Willy cried to go too, but it was too far for his little feet to trudge, or she would gladly have taken him. They watched her from the door till her figure lessened to a mere speck on the sand. How would she return to them,— with failure or success. They hardly dared to think!

Meantime, the little maid kept courageously on her way. The sun was high and hot, but a breath of coolness came from the waves which spilled themselves in long breakers of lazy brine along the edge of the sand. But she hardly noticed the heat, or the cool, whispering water; her eyes were fixed on the great building before her, which began to grow more distinct every moment. Windows, doors, chimneys, roofs, gables, columns, gradually disentangled themselves; and she saw knots of people here and there, and a crowd scattered on the long piazza; and before the house on the level green, youths and maidens, gayly clad, were playing tennis, careless of the sun. Like a soldier marching to battle, Peggy walked past these, straight up to one of the three broad flights of steps, the one at the left-hand entrance. She dared not look about her, for she felt many eyes upon her as she set her basket down on the lower step and took off the protecting newspapers, folding them for future use. She slipped the grandmother's old kerchief off her head, she was so warm, and began to climb the stairs slowly and with sinking heart. She stood still at last, with down-dropped eyes and blushing cheeks, feeling all the dreaded eyes upon her, and wishing she were a plover, to fly home by the breakers' edge. Suddenly a child's voice at her side said, "Oh, *look* at the pretty flowers, mamma! I want some; please buy some for me!" and a lovely lady in black spoke to her gently. Peggy started like a frightened sandpiper, though the lady only said, "How lovely your flowers are, my dear! May I have some? What is the price of this bunch of sweet peas?" and she drew a mass of fragrant scarlet flowers out of the basket, while the little girl who had begged stretched out both hands for them.

"Wait a minute, Minnie. How much are they?" she asked of Peggy.

"Twenty-five cents," Peggy ventured in answer; and the lady drew the coin from her purse and laid it in Peggy's happy palm. The contact seemed to give her new life, and her eyes grew moist with joy. She sent a swift glance out over the hot coast-line to where she knew her poor little home lay, a mere speck in the melting distance, but oh, how dear it seemed! And her hope grew strong and her fears less, and she held the precious piece of silver tight, lest it should take wings and fly away from her.

But now the contents of Peggy's basket began to disappear with surprising rapidity, faster and faster, till more than half her nosegays were sold, and she was quite breathless with joy. Nothing had ever looked so beautiful to her as the coins of silver she held in her hand, which soon grew too small to hold them all! They meant bread for her hungry dear ones; they meant joy for that little home saddened by poverty. She cared no more what people said, what they thought; she was sure of success for today; she held already help for tomorrow in her delighted hands.

"May I have this pansy for my buttonhole?" said a fine deep voice at her ear. She started, and turned and gave the speaker the last little bunch she had left. He put the flowers in their place, and took from the basket two bunches of white sweet peas and slipped the money into her hand.

"Tell me," he said very gently, "who taught you to put the colors in masses like these? Why do you do it?"

"I don't know," she answered; "they are prettier so," and she shyly proceeded to rearrange the nosegays she had left.

"Why do you put grass with the poppies?" he asked. "Did any one tell you to do it?"

"No," she said; "but I always think they belong together."

"Yes, they do, " he said; "but who told you so?"

"No one; they told me, themselves," she answered, smiling a little.

"Fortunate child!" he said; "they don't tell every one, though it's an open secret."

He was moving away, with his hands full of sweet peas, when he seemed to remember something, and came back.

"Will you come with me," he said," and bring your basket to a lady who is not strong enough to come so far down the piazza?"

Peggy followed silently, and in a sheltered corner, shaded carefully from the sun, she found one of the loveliest sights she had ever seen. A lady, sixty years old, perhaps, was lying back in a reclining chair, and about her several people sat quietly chatting. The lady's face was as fair as lilies, with eyes clear and undimmed by her sixty years. Her smile was sweeter than any smile Peggy had ever seen. Her hair was like silvered snow over her calm forehead, and she wore above this shining hair a little cap of lace as delicate as if woven of cobwebs and hoar-frost, with a bit of white satin ribbon like a moonbeam folded on the top.

"She is beautiful as my sweet peas," thought Peggy, as Mr. Willard put the flowers into her lovely hands; "they just suit her."

"I've brought you some posies, Mrs. Burton, as you see," said her friend; "and here is the little girl who knows all about them."

"Oh, how beautiful!" cried Mrs. Burton, in a delightful, sympathetic voice; "a thousand thanks!" And, turning to Peggy, "you brought them, my dear? Come nearer and let me see what else you have. Why, these are wonderful! Look at them, my daughter," she said to a sweet young girl who sat close beside her. "Why, Nelly, did you ever see anything like them? What color, what Oriental splendor! Where did you get them? Tell me, my child! I must have them all, every one; let me see, here are eight bouquets, five large and three smaller; twenty-five cents, did you say? Here it is; just two dollars. What is it, these small bunches only ten? Oh, never mind, I'm sure they're worth quite as much as the large ones. There, Nelly dear, that's for you, and this for you, and you, and you," she said, laughing delightfully, as she gave one to each person about her. "There, now, we all are happy, aren't we? And now, I wish to know all about these extraordinary flowers; sit down here, my dear, and tell me."

Peggy did as she was bid, though she longed to fly home, since her task was done for that day, but the lady had been so kind she could not refuse; indeed, no one could ever refuse *that* lady anything! When, by gentle questioning, she had won from Peggy all her story, she laid her hand on the little girl's bright hair with a beautiful gesture of affectionate protection; but she made no comment, she asked only, "Are you coming tomorrow, my dear, to bring some more flowers? Don't fail, for we all want them."

With joy Peggy answered, "Yes, indeed, I will come I."
"Remember, I wish a fresh bouquet every morning, and one for Nelly, too. Now, I know you're longing to get back; you shall go;" and Peggy took up her empty basket, her eyes bright with tears of delight.

"You dear child," said the sweet young lady whom her mother called Nelly, "did you wear no hat all that long way across the hot sand?"

"No," answered Peggy; "I didn't mind, I had my grandmother's handkerchief; it did very well," and she took it out of her pocket to tie again over her bright hair.

The younger lady reached behind her mother's chair and took a straw hat from where it hung by its strings, and quietly placed it on Peggy's head. It was a broad-brimmed hat of beautiful braided white straw; simply trimmed with some soft, white mull, light as the foam of the sea. The child could scarcely believe her ears when the lady said,

"There, dear, it's for you. Don't come out in the sun without it again!" and kissed her cheek. "Now, good-by. Don't say a word. Run home."

"Thank you, oh, thank you!" cried Peggy.

Run home? She did not run, she flew! She did not look behind her, she thought of nothing but the joy she was taking to those anxious hearts who were expecting her. As her swift steps covered the distance between her and that cottage of her love, she seemed to tread on air; she forgot she was hungry and hot and tired; she could not stop a moment to rest; while under the shade of the pretty hat her cheeks burned and eyes glistened with a joy too great to be told.

Meantime, the watchers in the cottage counted the moments of her absence; and when at last her slight figure became visible, yet a long, long way off, little Willy rushed forth to meet her.

"Stop, Willy, wait for me," his father cried, moving slowly down the steps. "Take hold of my hand, Willy; we'll go together." But she came so fast that the two slow walkers had gone only a short way before she caught up to them, quite breathless, and flung her arm~round her father's neck, and cried, "Oh, father, I sold them all!" throwing her empty basket as far as she could, till it rolled over and over on the sand, while she hugged him and kissed him again and again. And what a story she had to tell when in a few minutes they were all together again in the humble little room, and she spread out all her precious earnings on the table before them. There were eight dollars in silver pieces, it was incredible! What rejoicing, what happiness!

"Oh, mother!" cried Peggy, suddenly growing quite white, "I'm so hungry! Is there anything to eat?"

"My dear, my dear! Here is your bowl of porridge, the last oatmeal we have in the house. I saved it for you"; and she set it before the tired girl; for it was quite the middle of the afternoon, many hours since the scant breakfast. Well might she be hungry with all she had gone through.

"But, mother dear, as soon as I rest a little, I'll go up to the village for what we need."

"No, indeed, my darling, I will go; you mind the baby and rest all you can. But where did you get the beautiful hat?" And Peggy told, and there were smiles and tears, and kisses and congratulations afresh.

"Here's your kerchief all safe, grandmother dear," she said, taking it carefully out of her pocket.

"Oh, Peggy, you're a blessing to us!" the old woman sighed; "I always said you were not born on Sunday for nothing. And you are going with your flowers again to the hotel, tomorrow?"

"Yes, going again tomorrow," Peggy cried, all her terrors blown to the winds.

"My Margaret, my little Peggy, my brave girl!" her father said, with tender pride.

The group she had left at the hotel had watched her depart with no common interest.

"What a really beautiful creature!" Mr. Willard had said when she was out of hearing.

"Yes, and what a beautiful soul!" cried the enthusiastic old lady.

"Now, I am going to be that child's fairy godmother. That is settled! You shall see! She shall have everything she needs. She shall have all her people taken care of and put in the way of helping themselves, and she shall not be separated from them, for that would break her heart; but she shall have an education, and all her gifts and graces shall be cultivated for her own joy and the joy of all who come in contact with her!"

"I told her she was a fortunate child," said Mr. Willard, smiling, "but I hardly knew how fortunate; yet I think you are more fortunate in having the power to do these beautiful things."

"Why, what is the use of money but for such things?" she answered. "Of what good is my money to me if I cannot use it to make people better and happier?"

And so she did all that she promised herself she would do for Peggy and Peggy's family. She allowed her to go on selling the flowers while they lasted, watching her daily, growing to love her more and more, and to admire and respect her, as did all who came near her. Before the garden was exhausted, Peggy had made three hundred dollars for her father,— a fortune, it seemed to them all! No more fears for the winter now! At home they fairly worshiped her, and she was so happy that she no longer envied the song sparrow as it sang on the garden wall, the only bird that stays to sing the summer through. "I'm just as glad as you are," she said, as she watched it and listened to its sweet warble; and it turned its pretty head and looked at her with bright black eyes, as much as to say, "I know it, merry comrade, and you deserve it, too!"

And this is what grew in Peggy's garden. She planted more than the flowers. She sowed seeds of patience and meekness and faithfulness, courage and hope and love,— and glorious was the blossoming thereof.

# THE SANDPIPER'S NEST

IT was such a pretty nest, and in such a pretty place, that I must tell you about it.

One lovely afternoon in May I had been wandering up and down, through rocky gorges, by little swampy bits of ground, and on the tops of windy headlands, looking for flowers, and had found many: large blue violets, the like of which you never saw; white violets, too, creamy and fragrant; gentle little houstonias; gay and dancing erythroniums; and wind flowers delicately tinted, blue, straw-color, pink, and purple. I never found such in the mainland valleys. The salt air of the sea deepens the colors of all flowers. I stopped by a swamp which the recent rains had filled and turned into a little lake. Light green iris-leaves cut the water like sharp and slender swords, and, in the low sunshine that streamed across, threw long shadows over the shining surface. Some blackbirds were calling sweetly in a clump of bushes, and song sparrows sung as if they had but one hour in which to crowd the whole rapture of the spring. As I pressed through the budding bayberry bushes to reach some milk-white sprays of shadbush which grew by the water side, I startled three curlews. They flew away, trailing their long legs, and whistling fine and clear. I stood still to watch them out of sight. How full the air was of pleasant sounds! The very waves made a glad noise about the rocks, and the whole sea seemed to roar afar off, as if half asleep and murmuring in a kind of gentle dream. The flock of sheep was scattered here and there, all washed as white as snow by the plenteous rains, and nibbling the new grass eagerly; and from near and far came the tender and plaintive cries of the young lambs.

Going on again, I came to the edge of a little beach, and presently I was startled by a sound of such terror and distress that it went to my heart at once. In a moment a poor little sandpiper emerged from the bushes, dragging itself along in such a way that, had you seen it, you would have believed that every bone in its body had been broken. Such a dilapidated bird! Its wings drooped, and its legs hung as if almost lifeless. It uttered continually a shrill cry of pain, and kept just out of the reach of my hand, fluttering hither and thither as if sore wounded and weary. At first I was amazed, and cried out, "Why, friend and gossip! what's the matter?" and then stood watching it in mute dismay. Suddenly it flashed across me that this was only my sandpiper's way of concealing from me a nest; and I remembered reading about this little trick of hers in a book of natural history. The object was to make me follow her by pretending she could not fly, and so lead me away from her treasure. So I stood perfectly still, lest I should tread on the precious habitation, and quietly observed my deceitful little friend. Her apparently desperate and hopeless condition grew so comical when I reflected that it was only affectation, that I could not help laughing loud and long. "Dear gossip," I called to her, "pray don't give yourself so much unnecessary trouble You might know I wouldn't hurt you or your nest for the world, you most absurd of birds!" As if she understood me, and as if she could not brook being ridiculed, up she rose at once, strong and graceful, and flew off with a full, round, clear note, delicious to hear.

Then I cautiously looked for the nest, and found it quite close to my feet, near the stem of a stunted bayberry bush. Mrs. Sandpiper had only drawn together a few bayberry leaves, brown and glossy, a little pale green lichen, and a twig or two, and that was a pretty enough house for her. Four eggs about as large as robins' were within, all laid evenly with the small ends together, as is the tidy fashion of the Sandpiper family. No wonder I did not see them; for they were pale green like the lichen, with brown spots the color of the leaves and twigs, and they seemed a part of the ground, with its confusion of soft neutral tints. I could not admire them enough, but, to relieve my little friend's anxiety, I came very soon away, and as I came I marveled much that so very small a head should contain such an amount of cunning.